*Fiddling and dancing on a raft made from tree trunks that still have some of their branches, these rivermen display their talent for having a good time.*

COVER: *At the levee in New Orleans, the steamboats load for the journey upriver.*

FRONT ENDSHEET: *A peddler in a top hat presents his wares at an isolated farmhouse, trying to sell cloth, pans, and needles from his horse-drawn cart.*

CONTENTS PAGE: *The* Wyoming, *built in Philadelphia in 1857, was one of the gaudiest engines of its day, with surfaces covered in scrollwork and fancy brass.*

BACK ENDSHEET: *This lithograph shows a wood-burning locomotive built in 1856 by the Amoskeag Manufacturing Company of Manchester, New Hampshire.*

*"A knowledge of the past prepares us for the crisis of the present and the challenge of the future."*

JOHN F. KENNEDY
From his special foreword in Volume 1

# THE AMERICAN HERITAGE NEW ILLUSTRATED HISTORY OF THE UNITED STATES

## VOLUME 5

# YOUNG AMERICA

*By* ROBERT G. ATHEARN
*Professor of History, University of Colorado*

CREATED AND DESIGNED BY THE EDITORS OF
AMERICAN HERITAGE
*The Magazine of History*

PUBLISHED BY
DELL PUBLISHING CO., INC., NEW YORK

# CONTENTS OF THE COMPLETE SERIES

*Foreword by* JOHN F. KENNEDY
*Introduction by* ALLAN NEVINS
*Main text by* ROBERT G. ATHEARN

**Vol. 1   THE NEW WORLD**
*Special picture portfolios:*
THE SPANISH CONQUEST
THE PILGRIMS' EUROPE
*Special contributor:*
THOMAS F. McGANN—
THE ORDEAL OF CABEZA DE VACA

**Vol. 2   COLONIAL AMERICA**
*Special picture portfolios:*
THE FRENCH AND INDIAN WARS
LIFE IN COLONIAL AMERICA
*Special contributor:*
A. L. ROWSE—
THE PILGRIM AND PURITAN FATHERS

**Vol. 3   THE REVOLUTION**
*Special picture portfolios:*
THE DECLARATION OF INDEPENDENCE
THE ARMS AND THE MEN
*Special contributor:*
GEORGE F. SCHEER—
FRANCIS MARION: THE ELUSIVE SWAMP FOX

**Vol. 4   A NEW NATION**
*Special picture portfolios:*
THOMAS JEFFERSON
THE WAR AT SEA
*Special contributor:*
OLIVER JENSEN—
THE MANY-FACETED MR. PEALE

**Vol. 5   YOUNG AMERICA**
*Special picture portfolios:*
STIRRINGS OF INDUSTRY
NEW ROADS—THE WATERWAYS
*Special contributor:*
ARNOLD WHITRIDGE—
ELI WHITNEY: NEMESIS OF THE SOUTH

**Vol. 6   THE FRONTIER**
*Special picture portfolios:*
THE GREAT GOLD RUSH
INDIANS OF THE PLAINS
*Special contributor:*
STEPHEN W. SEARS—JEDEDIAH S. SMITH:
UNSUNG PATHFINDER OF THE WEST

**Vol. 7   WAR WITH MEXICO**
*Special picture portfolios:*
WAR IN THE WEST
WHALERS AND CLIPPERS
*Special contributor:*
GERALD W. JOHNSON—
DANIEL WEBSTER: GREAT MAN ELOQUENT

**Vol. 8   THE CIVIL WAR**
*Special picture portfolios:*
PRESIDENT LINCOLN
THE NAVAL WAR
*Special contributor:*
BRUCE CATTON—"HAYFOOT, STRAWFOOT!"

**Vol. 9   WINNING THE WEST**
*Special picture portfolios:*
COWBOYS—LIFE ON THE RANGE
THE LAST WARS WITH THE INDIANS
*Special contributor:*
STEWART H. HOLBROOK—
THE LEGEND OF JIM HILL

**Vol. 10   AGE OF STEEL**
*Special picture portfolios:*
MAKE WAY FOR THE IRON HORSE!
THE ROBBER BARONS
*Special contributor:*
JOHN A. GARRATY—
WILLIAM JENNINGS BRYAN

**Vol. 11   THE GILDED AGE**
*Special picture portfolios:*
THE ROMANTIC WORLD OF CURRIER AND IVES
THE VICTORIAN LOOK
*Special contributor:*
NELSON LANSDALE—
MRS. GARDNER AND HER PALACE

**Vol. 12   A WORLD POWER**
*Special picture portfolios:*
THE SPANISH-AMERICAN WAR
THE CITY GOES MODERN
*Special contributor:*
ROBERT L. HEILBRONER—
ANDREW CARNEGIE: EPITAPH FOR THE STEELMASTER

**Vol. 13   WORLD WAR I AND THE TWENTIES**
*Special picture portfolios:*
THE WAR IN THE AIR
AMERICA AS ADVERTISED
*Special contributor:*
ALLAN NEVINS—
HENRY FORD: A COMPLEX MAN

**Vol. 14   THE ROOSEVELT ERA**
*Special picture portfolios:*
F.D.R.
THE ARTIST'S AMERICA
*Special contributor:*
MERLO J. PUSEY—
F.D.R. VS. THE SUPREME COURT

**Vol. 15   WORLD WAR II**
*Special picture portfolios:*
D-DAY
THE UNITED NATIONS
*Special contribution:*
ONE WHO SURVIVED:
THE NARRATIVE OF ALLEN HEYN

**Vol. 16   AMERICA TODAY**
*Special picture portfolio:*
THE WORLD OF OUTER SPACE
*The Presidents and the Presidential elections*
*The Presidents and their cabinets*
*Index of the complete series*

A MASTER INDEX FOR ALL 16 VOLUMES APPEARS IN VOLUME 16

# CONTENTS OF VOLUME 5

Chapter 13. NATIONALISM RAMPANT          364

Chapter 14. THE JACKSONIANS              390

Chapter 15. SINEWS OF A NATION           422

SPECIAL PICTURE PORTFOLIOS:

   Stirrings of Industry                377

   New Roads—The Waterways            407

SPECIAL CONTRIBUTOR:

   ARNOLD WHITRIDGE

   Eli Whitney: Nemesis of the South      442

# NATIONALISM RAMPANT

The most important result of the War of 1812 was the improvement in Anglo-American diplomatic relations. Even though each side regarded the settlement as something of a truce, both were eager to avoid a renewal of hostilities. England wanted to be free of any dangers at her back so that she might expand her great domain overseas. The Americans wanted to develop their Western domain.

The first major postwar settlement between the two nations was the Rush-Bagot agreement, ratified by the United States Senate in 1818. Proposed by President Madison in 1817, it dealt with the armed vessels that both countries had put on the Great Lakes during the war. Charles Bagot, British minister to the United States, exchanged notes with Richard Rush, the acting Secretary of State, which provided that each power should have no more than a single-gun 100-ton vessel on Lake Champlain and Lake Ontario, and two such vessels on Erie, Huron, Michigan, and Superior. The

*This turbulent election day in Philadelphia in the autumn of 1815 was painted by German-born artist John Lewis Krimmel.*

basic agreement is still in effect today, although by mutual consent there have been occasional modifications over the years.

Encouraged by this agreement, the two nations resolved other differences in the Convention of 1818. Right after the war Great Britain had maintained that our fishing privileges in Canadian waters, gained at the Treaty of 1783, were no longer in effect. The diplomats now agreed that fishing rights should be restored. Another unsettled difficulty concerned the Canadian-American border. The northern boundary of the Louisiana Purchase was still undefined, and although there seemed to be little chance that the area would soon be populated, both sovereignties were glad to settle on the 49th parallel for the part of the boundary between the Lake of the Woods in northern Minnesota and the Rocky Mountains. West of the Rockies, the border country was held in joint occupancy until the settlement of 1846.

The Convention of 1818 also took up the matter of American slaves carried off by the British during the War of 1812. Czar Alexander of Russia was asked to mediate, and by 1822 he submitted a recommendation awarding the United States $1,200,000 compensation for the slaves and for other debts that the British had incurred.

### Dealings with Spain

The United States now turned to Spain to settle some long-standing territorial questions concerning the Floridas. American interest in that region dated back to the foundation of the Republic, and with the Louisiana Purchase, there was renewed interest in rounding out our holdings. East and West Florida not only plunged deep into the Caribbean, affecting sea connections with Louisiana, but they also controlled the mouths of navigable streams in the present states of Mississippi and Alabama.

At first the Americans tried to bluff the Spanish. Robert Livingston, who negotiated the Louisiana Purchase, knew perfectly well that it did not include the Floridas, but he pretended to so construe it. When Jefferson left office, he spoke of making Florida and Cuba a part of the Union. Later, in 1810, Madison made no objection when a group of American settlers in West Florida staged a revolt and proclaimed the Republic of Florida. In fact, when the settlers asked admittance to the United States, Madison extended American authority to West Florida. Naturally, the Spanish protested, but they were deeply involved in war and could do little to enforce

their objections. Nor could their British allies help, for they, too, were in a death struggle with Napoleon. International reaction to the Florida affair was summarized by the Russian czar. When the American minister tried to explain the situation to him, he merely bowed and remarked with a smile, "Everybody is getting a little bigger nowadays."

Meanwhile, Negro slaves escaped into Spanish territory with increasing frequency, as did Seminole Indians fleeing from federal troops. The inevitable crisis came in 1818. Andrew Jackson chased some of the Indians across the international border and then hanged two Englishmen, whom he accused of inciting them. The execution of Alexander Arbuthnot and Robert Ambrister angered the British, and along with the Spanish minister to Washington, they registered a sharp protest.

John Quincy Adams, Secretary of State, suggested to the Spanish that one solution of the difficulty was for the United States to buy the Floridas. After lengthy negotiations, Spain agreed, and on February 22, 1819, relinquished her claim to both East and West Florida. The Adams-Onis Treaty, named for the two negotiators, also defined the western boundary of the Louisiana Purchase and strengthened American claims to Oregon as the Spanish surrendered all rights in that territory. For all this the United States gave $5,000,000 and then agreed to make no claim to Texas

*The Rush-Bagot agreement limited the number of American and British armed vessels on each of the Great Lakes. This one is at Fort Malden, Ontario.*

as a result of the Louisiana Purchase.

With almost no military effort, America had settled some troublesome problems and made some significant changes in the size of the country. Generally, the proponents of nationalism were pleased. A few, like Henry Clay, thought the United States had not gone far enough. He had wanted Texas, too. The next few decades were to realize the wildest dreams of such land-hungry men.

Successful negotiations with England and Spain during the postwar years enhanced the American feeling of equality among nations. Suddenly the country emerged as a national entity, somewhat gawky and self-conscious but aware of its relative strength in the Western Hemisphere. Residents of the young land acquired a new, shoulder-swinging pride that probably annoyed the Europeans, but they were much too busy recovering from their recent conflict to restrain the youthful upstart.

From the standpoint of size, the United States posed no threat to any of the older countries. Its population was about 10,000,000 and not more than 600,000 square miles were settled, as compared to 3,000,000 today. The Union was a confederation of 24 loosely joined states, only two of them west of the Mississippi River, each still jealous of its own powers

*Law on the frontier was most often a matter of an individual's power, but as settlements grew, courts were established. This 1849 painting shows a rural session where, obviously, the solemnity of the court is not being fully felt.*

despite the currents of nationalism that were beginning to flow strongly.

After 1815, Americans were primarily concerned with domestic problems, both economic and political. They tended to turn their backs upon Europe and to look toward the undeveloped West. They rationalized their new orientation by rereading Thomas Paine's *Common Sense,* or by referring to George Washington's Farewell Address. Both men had warned that Europe and America had separate interests. Even the internationally minded Jefferson took this view in his later years. Out of this type of thinking grew the Monroe Doctrine, a theory of hemispheric isolation that was to polarize American foreign policy for a century.

The immediate reason for the doctrine's enunciation was the state of affairs in Europe. Spain, now weak and poor, was struggling to recover her South American colonies, lost by revolt during the era of the Napoleonic Wars. The Russians, Austrians, and French, deeply affected by postwar conservatism, wanted the Spanish colonies restored to their former owner. The British did not agree. After years of turmoil, England's economy was now expanding internationally, and she did not want to lose her new-found trade with such young Hispanic-American nations as Argentina and Venezuela. For years she had sought to enter those restricted markets, and now her Continental neighbors were about to deny her the fruits of her patience.

George Canning, England's foreign minister, looked around for support. He knew he was opposed by most of the other European powers in his wish to see the independence of the South American nations maintained. But he also knew the United States was opposed to any further European encroachments in the Western Hemisphere. Therefore, he turned to Richard Rush, the American minister at London, and suggested that the mother and daughter stand against any such invasion. Rush, in turn, sent the proposal to President Monroe, who promptly asked advice from his cabinet and from two old friends, Jefferson and Madison.

## The Monroe Doctrine—by Adams

Both ex-Presidents advised Monroe to cooperate with the British, but Secretary of State John Quincy Adams was against it. He argued that the United States should stand alone. He knew Great Britain valued American friendship, particularly for commercial reasons. He was sure England would oppose France and the others, with or without cooperation from this side of the Atlantic. Resting his case upon these facts, he felt his country could safely act alone and need not

be a junior partner to England. As he said, "It would be more candid as well as more dignified, to avow our principles explicitly to Russia and to France, than to come in as a cockboat in the wake of the British man-of-war."

So the Monroe administration elected to hoist its own colors and sail the waters of international affairs independently. In his annual message in 1823, Monroe enunciated what was later known as his doctrine. Its sentiments, found scattered all through the message, warned Europe that the Hispanic-American nations were independent and no longer subject to colonization by foreign powers. He reiterated Washington's position that the Europeans had interests different from ours and that we would resist any attempt on their part to extend their system to this hemisphere. He also assured the world that we had no interest in interfering with any existing European colonies on this side of the Atlantic and promised that we would refrain from interfering in European wars that did not involve us.

The message, well received in the United States, brought various reactions from Europe. The English, in general, were pleased. The Austrians and Russians were furious, the French were divided, and the Spanish seemed unconcerned. The American ambassador to Madrid was dumfounded at the lack of interest in a document so vital to Spain. Also surprising was the lack of comment from South America. Although Latin Americans appreciated an interest in their welfare, they no more wanted interference from the United States than they wanted it from the powers of Europe.

## The Era of Good Feelings

The growing spirit of nationalism in postwar America was shown at home as well as abroad. While the diplomats were busy molding an American foreign policy, their countrymen turned the land into a hive of economic activity. It was the day of the turnpike, the canal, and the earliest railroads. In the Northwest, frontiersmen hacked away at the wilderness, clearing new holdings, building settlements, and driving back the Indian population. In the South, an empire known as the Cotton Kingdom was developing fast, tremendously stimulated by Eli Whitney's 1793 invention of a machine to separate seeds from cotton.

The years following the War of 1812 were characterized as the Era of Good Feelings. The Democratic-Republicans (as the party of Jefferson, Madison, and Monroe was called until about 1828, when it became the Democratic Party) were still in power, as the Federalists had dug their political graves by fruitless opposition to the war. A predominantly Democratic-Republican Congress passed America's first protective tariff in 1816, taking its lead from Hamilton's earlier *Report on Manufacturing*. They also stole Federalist thunder by rechartering the Bank of the United States in 1816. Foreign-policy questions, once a main point of difference between the two parties, were no longer in the forefront. Napoleon was exiled to St. Helena, and Europe was busy restoring its unemployed monarchs to their former positions. In general, with Democratic-Republicans acting and talking like Federalists, there seemed to be little occasion for further factional strife on the political scene.

## The indomitable John Marshall

Yet in this predominantly Jeffersonian era, it was a Federalist who led the nationalists in establishing a strong central government. John Marshall firmly believed that the United States was a federal unit, not a confederation or an association of states that grudgingly allotted power to the central government. Early in his career as Chief Justice, he gave warning that he held far-reaching judicial opinions. His verdict in the 1803 case of *Marbury vs. Madison,* asserting that the court had the power to declare the laws of Congress unconstitutional, marked out the field of battle.

The decade following the War of 1812 saw Marshall at his best. His quick sense of humor, his lack of pretension, and his democratic conduct with his associates won their respect. They chuckled over the story of a Richmond resident who approached the shabbily dressed Chief Justice and, thinking him out of work, offered him a coin to carry a bundle. Much amused, Marshall gravely took the

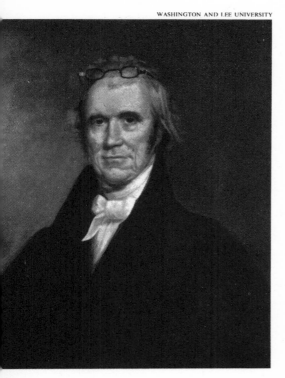

*John Marshall was the third Chief Justice, but he established the court's prestige.*

bundle and meekly padded along behind his new employer, to the delight of those who knew him.

During the postwar years, Marshall handed down decision after decision that strengthened the position of the federal judiciary. Earlier, in 1810, he had denied the state legislature of Georgia the privilege of rescinding a contract to sell some land. In 1819, the Dartmouth College case presented a similar question. The state legislature attempted to amend a charter given to the college in colonial days, in order to have some control over its operations. Marshall held that the charter was a contract, that the col-

lege was not a civil institution participating in government, and that the legislature had no right to intervene. The modern significance is that the charter of a corporation is considered to be a contract, as that word is used in the Constitution.

Marshall came to grips even more directly with the states in cases like that of *Cohens vs. Virginia* (1821). In this complicated case, Marshall sided with Virginia, but he took the opportunity to express his opinion of the nature of the Union. He made clear the supremacy of the federal judiciary over any state judiciary, even though it might agree with a state court's opinion.

Maryland also tried to defy the Chief Justice. In 1819, it passed a law providing that if a branch of the Bank of the United States were established in that state without permission, its notes would be taxed. The federal case that resulted, *McCulloch vs. Maryland,* was perhaps Marshall's greatest. The decision of the Supreme Court denied the right of a state to tax an agency of the central government, and Marshall used the case to further define the government's position: "Let the end be legitimate, let it be within the scope of the Constitution, and all means which are appropriate, which are plainly adapted to that end, which are not prohibited, but consistent with the letter and the spirit of the Constitution, are constitutional," wrote the Chief Justice in what is perhaps the best definition of implied powers we

371

have. In stating "The power to tax involves the power to destroy," he pointed out the dangers of placing state sovereignty above that of the federal government.

In such cases, Marshall struck at powers claimed by individual states—powers that he regarded as an invasion of the government's jurisdiction. In other rulings, he stepped forward, staking out new claims for the government, establishing precedents that would enhance its prestige. The most famous of these is *Gibbons vs. Ogden,* in which the court asserted the power of the government to regulate interstate commerce. The contest centered upon Ogden, who was trying to prevent Gibbons from operating rival steamboats between New York City and the New Jersey ports. Ogden claimed he had a monopoly from the state that gave him a prior right over Gibbons, who had a federal license. Marshall's ruling, in 1824, was that Ogden was wrong—that Congress had the power to regulate commerce whenever it crossed state boundaries.. He

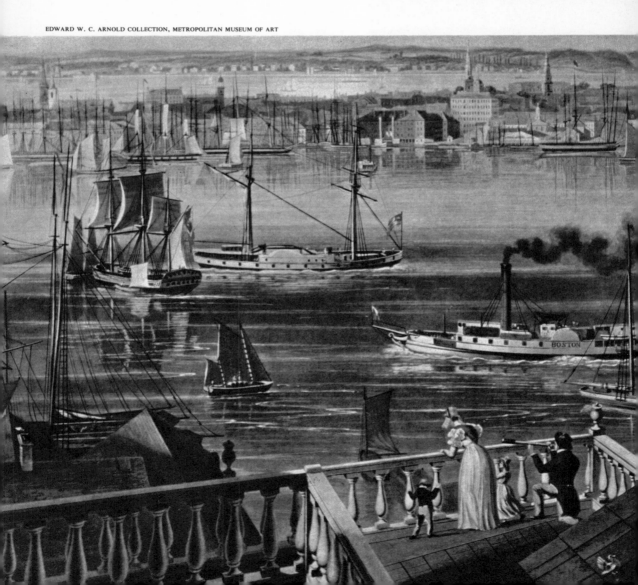

held that such jurisdiction affected passengers as well as goods. It was a decision of far-reaching implications. It set a precedent for subsequent governmental control over railroads, airlines, telephone and telegraph companies, power lines, and radio and television transmission.

Another case affecting commerce on the national level was that of *Brown vs. Maryland,* argued in 1827. The Chief Justice ruled that as long as goods imported into any state from abroad remained in the hands of the importer in the original package, they were not subject to state tax. The so-called Original-Package Case implied that a state's attempt to tax such packages was an attempt to regulate the nation's foreign commerce, a right reserved to the central government.

Decisions of such magnitude and implication naturally provoked criticism from the guardians of states'

*The area of dispute in the case of* Gibbons vs. Ogden *is shown in this 1837 view of New York from Brooklyn Heights with the shores of New Jersey in the distance.*

rights. A Senator from Kentucky, for example, passionately charged that the court was a "place above the control of the will of the people, in a state of disconnection with them, inaccessible to the charities and sympathies of human life."

Despite such complaints, most of Marshall's decisions fitted the spirit of nationalism pervading America in the early 19th century. They were also in agreement with the economic expansion of the day. Growing America, whose vast stretches were being interlaced by a transportation network, did not complain when court decisions favored its development. Men were making fortunes from young and lusty industries, and it was only natural that they wanted to retain their gains. If the Supreme Court appeared to be emerging as the stronghold of conservative America, businessmen gave it their blessing.

### Underlying sectionalism

In the American air of nationalism there was a throbbing beat of sectionalism that would one day rise to a crescendo and become the major theme. On the surface of everyday events, the dominant feature of national life appeared to be its magnificent expansion. New states came quickly into the Union after the War of 1812—six of them in six years. But so fast was the country developing that the result was weakness rather than strength. New England became a strong commercial empire in itself.

The Northwest, agricultural in the main, grew jealous of its own interests. And the South, where cotton was king, developed a sectional pride that transcended national feeling. As Frederick Jackson Turner, the great historian of the American frontier, put it, the country was dividing itself into vast physiographic provinces. Each felt itself in competition with another part of the nation, convinced that the central government favored one or more of its rivals.

John C. Calhoun, later to represent the most rabid of the sectionalists, showed concern at the growing divisions of interest as early as 1817. "We are greatly and rapidly—I was about to say fearfully—growing," he remarked. "This is our pride and our danger; our weakness and our strength." This was the same Calhoun who within a decade was complaining that the system of separate geographical areas was not sufficiently recognized.

The pressure of dissent was by no means centered in the South. During the years after 1815, the West was in the normal financial turmoil that any frontier area experiences. Money was scarce, land prices were a subject of complaint, and the internal-improvement program moved much too slowly for Westerners eager for land and trade. The panic of 1819 brought the condition into sharp focus, resulting in a storm of protest from the frontiersmen. They were momentarily silenced by the land law of 1820, which

*Marshall and the other six members of the Supreme Court appear on the dais at the left rear of the House of Representatives, as painted by S.F.B. Morse in 1822.*

cut the minimum cost to $1.25 an acre and the minimum acreage they could buy to 80. This law was meant to help the small farmer acquire land, but the provision substituting cash payment for the customary credit soured the new terms. Even if a Westerner now could buy a farm for $100, that amount of cash was hard to come by. East-West antagonisms were multiplying to such an extent that only a larger, and more dramatic, irritation could submerge the trouble.

It appeared before long. Ironically, it came from one aspect of America's exuberant nationalism—the rapid expansion. At the birth of the national government in 1789, the population balance between North and South was almost even; by 1819, the scales had shifted. There were over 5,000,000 people in the North to about 4,500,000 in the South. Although representation in the Senate stayed even, the House had 105 Northern Representatives to 81 Southerners. The question of political power, soon to be contested by these two great sections, first came to a test in neither of them. Missouri, then a frontier territory, was the crucible in which the elements of the coming battle were fused.

The people of Missouri applied for admission to the Union in 1818, and their request was referred to Congress. A New York Representative, James Tallmadge, moved that the request be granted. He introduced an amendment, however, providing that no more slaves would be introduced

375

into the new state and that all children born into slavery in Missouri after its admission to the Union should become free at the age of 25. With that, the fat was in the fire. The amendment passed the House but lost in the Senate, and in the process became an issue of national interest. Southerners at once maintained that Congress could not pose conditions for the entrance of new states, and Northerners answered by citing such examples as Ohio, Indiana, and Illinois, whose people had to observe stipulations laid down in the Northwest Ordinance. The sixth article of that document had prohibited slavery.

The question of Missouri's statehood appeared in Congress again in the fall of 1819 and continued into the winter, with Congressmen from each major section hurling oratorical thunderbolts right and left. At the height of the excitement, residents of that part of Massachusetts known as Maine asked permission to form a state. Politicians now conceived the idea of carrying Missouri into the Union on the back of Maine. Arguments over the slave issue were temporarily resolved when Senator Jesse Thomas of Illinois proposed the famous "36–30" amendment, whereby slavery would be permitted in Missouri but prohibited elsewhere north of 36° 30′ latitude. It was the heart of the final settlement. By the spring of 1820, Maine was admitted as a free state, and after more than a year of additional wrangling, Missouri came into the Union on the terms of the Thomas amendment.

While most proslavery men then felt that Congress could prohibit slavery on land the government owned and out of which states would come, they continued to insist it could not impose conditions upon states when they sought admission to the Union. John Quincy Adams, a New England·er, thought they were right. It was he who shrewdly observed, "The discussion of the Missouri question disclosed a secret; it revealed the basis for a new organization of parties. Here was a new party ready-formed—terrible to the whole Union, but portentously terrible to the South." Although the new party—the Republican —would not be formed until 1854, the issue had now arisen, and for the next three decades the elements of a great national struggle would, one by one, fall into place.

Thus the Era of Good Feelings was in some respects a misnomer. The principal current of America's progress during the years following the War of 1812 emphasized expansion, the growth of the central government's power, and economic development. But strong undercurrents and eddies of sectional discord indicated that nationalism was merely the surface manifestation of the young and ebullient nation. Under this bright surface was a turmoil of conflicting emotions. Not many years hence they would burst forth upon a startled world as the American Civil War.

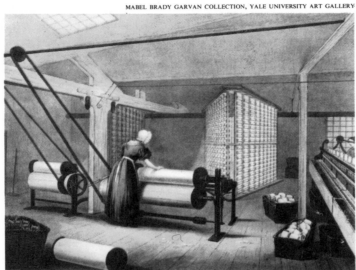

# STIRRINGS
# OF INDUSTRY

The Industrial Revolution that had swept England in the 18th century came late to America, a country that had been mainly concerned with agriculture. It was in the early 19th century that the United States began to settle the problems involved in simply existing as a new nation and to set about producing its own goods for consumption, such as textiles for clothing, machinery for farming, and vehicles for transportation. The beginnings of industry were difficult. Americans lacked the means to process raw materials and were slow to respond to the conceptions of men like Peter Cooper and Robert Fulton. But it was not long before the American mind ably applied itself to the challenge of industry. It was in the early activities of the men in this portfolio—men of imagination, courage, and conviction—that the seeds of industrial America were sown that have resulted in today's great mechanized society.

# WHEELS TURN

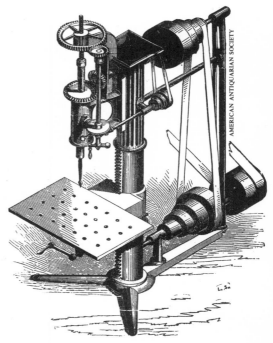

AMERICAN ANTIQUARIAN SOCIETY

Eli Whitney's revolutionary cotton gin, a device to remove seeds from cotton, is operated (above, left) on a plantation.

Mass production, the American industrial development that would one day sweep the world, was born in the Connecticut factory above. Here, in 1798, Eli Whitney used the machines he had invented, like the drill press (right), to make interchangeable parts, assembled later into rifles.

New England textile mills (left) mushroomed as bales of cotton from the gins of the South poured into Northern cities.

379

# AMERICA'S FIRST FACTORY

In 1789, Samuel Slater (above), a cotton spinner's apprentice with ambition and a good memory, slipped out of England and came to the United States with a valuable secret locked in his head. He had memorized the designs of England's most modern and carefully guarded textile machinery. (He could not risk drawing plans of it, for this was a criminal offense in England.) In the tall, narrow building (left), Moses Brown's mill in Pawtucket, Rhode Island, Slater struggled, with two machinists and a wheelwright, to make the intricate Arkwright spinning frame below. In 1790, this equipment went into operation, and the first factory in the United States was turning out spindles of cotton yarn.

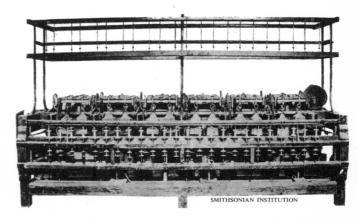

# STEAM MOVES IN

Oliver Evans (above) and Robert Fulton (below) were both pioneers in harnessing the great energy of the new steam engine.

Evans and Fulton suffered the fate of most visionaries—the snickers and the gibes of those who couldn't imagine ships without sails and horseless carriages. Although Evans' steam-powered Orukter Amphibolos (amphibious dredge) at the left looked strange indeed in 1803, it worked—and on land and water. Fulton, a talented painter as well as a brilliant engineer, was determined to prove to an age devoted to sailing ships that steam would propel ships of the future. His steamship *Clermont* (above) lacked the grace of a clipper ship, but in 1807 it successfully puffed its way up the Hudson River from New York City to Albany.

TWINE BINDER 1883

In This Field
July 25 1831
Will be tried a new
PATENT GRAIN CUTTER
invented
C. H. McCORMICK

STIRRINGS OF INDUSTRY

# McCORMICK'S REAPER

The American farm moved toward mechanization in 1831, when Cyrus McCormick's reaper was first demonstrated successfully in a wheat field in Virginia. Incredulous onlookers saw the horsepowered implement cut six times as much grain in a day as a single farm hand could cut with a scythe.

385

Peter Cooper was one of America's first great industrialists and a New York civic leader.

# THE TRAIN
# TAKES OVER

In 1830, Cooper's one-horsepower railroad steam engine, the *Tom Thumb,* pulled a car of spectators (below) in a race with a horse-drawn car. Although the horse won this race because of a mechanical failure in the engine, the inventor had convinced many people that railways were the transportation of the future. Within a few decades, cars hauled by puffing locomotives (above) would supersede covered wagons in America's Far West.

The steel for America's first locomotives was forged at the West Point

Foundry, which began to work iron in 1818 in Cold Spring, New York.

# CHAPTER 14

# THE JACKSONIANS

The currents of conflict beneath the surface of the Era of Good Feelings began to break into the open as the election of 1824 drew near.

Before that election, New Englanders had watched the South maintain political dominance with an unbroken string of Virginians as successful Presidential candidates. Now their hope lay in a member of the old Adams family, John Quincy, whose reputation might bring the Presidency to a New Englander. He did not appeal to the frontier as a backwoodsman would have, but neither did he represent the Federalists of the commercial class. He was broadly educated, with wide experience in the diplomatic field, and his character was impeccable. Historian Frederick Jackson Turner says that Adams had Puritan restraint, self-scrutiny, and self-condemnation. Adams' own self-assessment was "I am a man of reserved, cold, austere, and forbidding manners."

Adams' quest for the Presidency was not an easy one. A number of widely popular political figures on the scene offered him sharp competition. Henry Clay, Speaker of the House—known as Harry of the West—had a large following, as did a fellow Westerner, Andrew Jackson. Southerners like William Crawford of Georgia and John C. Calhoun of South Carolina were also contenders.

Adams regarded Clay and Jackson with distaste. Clay, a Kentuckian, represented a way of life that a proper New Englander like Adams found objectionable. Clay was fond of horse racing, had no objection to the social glass, and played both poker and politics with enthusiasm and skill. His manner pleased many voters, and his ability as a compromiser and his interest in internal improvements pleased others. Andrew Jackson was even more Western than Clay. Those who worshiped the hero of New Orleans crossed all party lines and geographical boundaries.

Such competition did not deter Adams, who quietly built support as his followers reminded voters of his achievements as Secretary of State under Monroe. The acquisition of Florida in 1819, and Spain's relin-

*Andrew Jackson, painted here by Alonzo Chappel, became a national hero after defeating the British at New Orleans in 1815.*

*John Quincy Adams, though capable, was a frustrated President.*

quishment of its claims north of the 42nd parallel, attributed to Adams' diplomacy, gained him favor.

The Missouri Compromise, which Adams referred to as a "flaming sword," politically affected all the aspirants. Crawford lost strength by his states'-rights stand; Clay's compromises cost him votes in both the North and the South; Calhoun, a Southerner, likewise suffered. Jackson was the least affected. During the height of the Missouri controversy he was busy in Florida fighting Indians and hanging Englishmen, an undertaking that had strong appeal to the nationalist voter.

Adams, however, actually benefited from the Missouri Compromise; it helped to install him as the Northern candidate. Privately he condemned slavery; publicly he had, for constitutional reasons, opposed any restrictions upon Missouri's entrance into the Union—a stand that had Southerners applauding.

When the 1824 election results were in, Jackson had 99 electoral votes, and Adams had 84. Because neither had a majority, the contest was thrown into the House of Representatives as is provided for in the Twelfth Amendment. Clay, who had run last, now threw his support to Adams, who was elected.

When Clay was appointed Secretary of State, the cry of corruption was raised. John Randolph of Virginia complained publicly to such an extent that he found himself in a duel with Clay. As they were both poor shots, the affray ended with no casualties. Jackson, although himself somewhat given to duels, kept his pistols encased and grimly planned his next battle—the election of 1828.

The administration of John Quincy Adams was generally unsatisfactory, and no one was more disappointed in it than the President himself. Although his previous success had been in diplomacy, he now found his foreign-affairs program the most seriously blocked. The United States Congress, filled with Adams' enemies, including many Jackson supporters, did little to help him. When the President wanted to send representatives to an international meeting held at Panama, Congress debated so long over their appointment that America was not represented. Great Britain, meanwhile, was represented thoroughly and lost no time in furthering commercial relationships with South America.

Adams tried to contain his dissatisfaction, but having cast aside the practice of distributing government jobs in return for support, he had no weapon with which to maintain control. Other men might use personal magnetism, but Adams had none. Lonely and introspective, he confided more and more in his beloved diary.

## The return of Andy Jackson

After Jackson's defeat in the Presidential contest of 1824–25, he resigned his seat in Congress and spent the next three years readying himself for the battle of 1828. His efforts, aided by Adams' failure, were successful. His victory in the election was overwhelming, and early in 1829 he made his return to Washington.

On Inauguration Day the capital was jammed with milling crowds. Daniel Webster made the gloomy remark that "They seem to think the country is rescued from some dreadful danger." He and others recoiled as roughhewn Jackson admirers jostled one another in the White House, upsetting pails of orange punch, breaking glasses, and climbing on the furniture with their muddy boots for a better look at Old Hickory.

The people's hero was now in power, and the people demanded a share of the victory. The lower classes

*Jackson's many executions of army deserters and his destruction of personal enemies were attacked in this 1828 cartoon.*

felt that rotation in office was not only part of the political game but that it was in keeping with the democratic principle of government.

Jackson agreed. Historically, he has been charged with starting the spoils system. He did not invent it, nor did he make excessive use of it. From George Washington's time it was customary to appoint to office one's supporters. Jackson's successors to the Presidency were to make him look as if he showed no favoritism at all when it came to handing out political jobs.

Old Hickory was typically Western in his informality. As soon as he was in office, the nation witnessed a sample of this method. Turning to his closest friends, the President gathered around him an unofficial group referred to derisively by his enemies as the "kitchen cabinet," and here national policy was made. The kitchen cabinet, chosen by Jackson wholly without partisan considerations, functioned smoothly enough, but the official cabinet soon became a problem that threatened the very existence of the new regime. A woman was at the bottom of the trouble. Her name was Peggy O'Neale Timberlake Eaton, and her place in American politics is unique.

The petticoat war started January 1, 1829, when Jackson's Tennessee friend and future Secretary of War, John H. Eaton, married Peggy, once a barmaid. An attractive young widow of a navy purser who had never returned from sea, she was an old friend of Andy Jackson's. Eaton had known Peggy well when she was still married to her first husband. Some accounts say that he married her on Jackson's advice in order to quiet gossipers.

It was Mrs. John C. Calhoun, wife of the Vice-President, who led the assault. She refused to call on Eaton's bride and made it clear that she considered the former Mrs. Timberlake unqualified to hold the social position into which she had married. The other cabinet wives, as well as a number of Washington ladies who were engaged in the struggle for prestige, joined up for the duration.

The free-for-all that ensued might have done little harm had not male reserves been called up. In the midst of the fray was Vice-President John Calhoun, who, wanting to be Presi-dent, believed he had only to wait for his chance to succeed to that office. But he became impatient and tried to increase the odds in his favor. There were two or three members of Jackson's cabinet whom he regarded as enemies. One was Secretary of State Martin Van Buren, who was also a Presidential possibility. Behind him stood John Eaton and William Barry, the Postmaster General. By helping to create an incident out of Eaton's choice of a wife, Calhoun hoped to break up the cabinet, embarrass the administration, and so improve his chances for the Presidency.

The plan worked well enough at first. The gallant Van Buren rushed to Peggy's defense, his own arm extended in proffered support at all social functions. Some say this simple gesture made him President of the United States, for Jackson was enormously pleased by such open loyalty.

If Calhoun was out to wreck the cabinet for his own purposes, Van Buren was out to perform an act of political judo, using the momentum of his opponent's assault to gain victory for himself. Accordingly, one day in the spring of 1831 he suggested his own resignation. He presumed this would cause Eaton to follow, as evidence of his loyalty to Jackson, whereupon the other cabinet members, no matter how reluctant they

*Symbols of Henry Clay's statecraft (right) and his life as a farmer are included in this life-size portrait by John Neagle.*

*Jackson's Indian policy forced most Eastern tribes across the Mississippi over what became known as the Trail of Tears.*

were, would feel they must resign also.

The scheme worked to perfection, and before long Jackson had the opportunity to reconstruct his cabinet, free from any Calhoun influence. Van Buren was rewarded with an appointment as minister to England, but the Senate, with Vice-President Calhoun casting the deciding vote, blocked his confirmation. This only heightened his popularity and standing in the Democratic Party, and the result was his immediate nomination and election to the Vice-Presidency on the Jackson ticket in 1832. He was now the heir apparent to Jackson's political crown. All he had to do was wait quietly until 1836. In 1832, Calhoun had resigned the Vice-Presidency to go back home and, as Senator, carry on the fight.

## Old Hickory loses some supporters

Before Jackson had been long in office, some Westerners began to wonder if the hero of New Orleans was as much their man as they had once thought. As Senator he had voted for federal support of such improvements as roads and canals in the American interior. As President he veered toward the strict constructionist point of view that some projects merited government assistance but that many more were too local to justify it. In improvements to river navigation, for example, he held that only projects benefiting two or more states could be considered of national importance and would get his support.

Before long there came before him a bill proposing a federal grant of $150,000 to aid in the construction of a road between Maysville, Kentucky, and the Ohio River, right through the heart of Jackson country and connecting Kentucky with the East. To the dismay of Westerners, the President vetoed the bill. In his veto message Jackson argued that the proposed road was to run altogether within the limits of a state, "conferring partial instead of general advantages."

The storm of protest was answered by the President's defenders, who pointed out that on the day of the veto—May 31, 1830—he approved a $130,000 expenditure to survey and extend the Cumberland Road running west from Maryland through Pennsylvania, Ohio, Indiana, and Illinois.

Jackson insisted that he was not hostile to internal improvements, if they were of national scope.

As for land and monetary policies, subjects on which Westerners were particularly touchy, Jackson also perplexed his fellows. Although he was an advocate of paper money, so popular among the inflation-minded frontiersmen, the President began to grow concerned about its extensive circulation. By the early 1830s, Western banks were printing unbacked paper money at a rate that threatened economic stability, and so rampant was the speculation that Jackson stepped in with federal control. In an order of July 11, 1836, called the Specie Circular, he dealt Westerners a severe blow by decreeing that public lands could be bought only with hard money, or specie. Western banks were the hardest hit, and in the financial contraction that followed, many were forced to close. Land sales fell off. When the panic came in 1837, frontiersmen were quick to blame the Specie Circular. So loud were the complaints that the order was withdrawn in 1838.

In other respects, Jackson's land policy pleased his farmer neighbors. During the years he was in office, almost 64,000,000 acres of public domain were disposed of by means of individual sales and grants to the states. In 1832, the President declared that public lands ought not to be used as a source of revenue, but should be sold at a price that barely covered administrative costs. The American government was now headed toward a policy of free land—a policy that would be realized in the Homestead Act of 1862.

In Indian affairs, Jackson held closer to the viewpoint that Americans expected of him. At the time of his administration, the Cherokees were the only powerful Indians remaining in well-settled parts of the country. Their lands in Georgia posed a problem, for although the federal government had long since recognized Cherokee property rights, the state government had annexed the tribal lands in 1828.

Jackson recommended to the Indians that they move peaceably across the Mississippi, where they would be granted new lands. The Cherokees said no. They ignored the tomahawk and, in a most savage manner, went straight to the Supreme Court of the United States. Startled, it backed away, asserting that the Indians could not sue there. A missionary named Samuel A. Worcester then arranged to bring the matter before the court in his name. In *Worcester vs. Georgia* (1832), John Marshall held that the federal government alone had jurisdiction in the domain of the Cherokee nation, and therefore the Georgia law was unconstitutional.

Georgia ignored the ruling, and when all concerned turned to Jackson for an answer, he roared, "John Marshall has made his decision, now let him enforce it." The Indians saw they were beaten and agreed to move westward, where more land and a settlement of $5,000,000 awaited them. Other tribes made similar agreements, and during Jackson's administration they journeyed over what they called the Trail of Tears to a new home.

### Jackson and the Southerners

Back in the early 1820s, the South was, in general, safely national in viewpoint. Yet only 10 years were to elapse before those insisting upon states' rights would become dominant and even gain complete control of one state, South Carolina. This represented the beginning of the most serious internal conflict the United States had faced until then—a conflict that was not to be settled until the nation fought the Civil War.

The friction between the federal government and the states'-righters in South Carolina began over the tariff of 1828, which they wanted to nullify. The notion that a state could nullify a national law that it regarded as unconstitutional was not new. The Kentucky and Virginia Resolutions of 1798 had stressed the "compact" theory of government, contending that Congress had transcended its powers by passing the Alien and Sedition Acts. In 1828, Calhoun expounded a strong states'-rights position in a pamphlet called *The South Carolina Exposition and Protest*. More excitement might have resulted if the author's identity had been revealed, but it was not. The main theme of this

document was that a state might annul a law of Congress that it regarded as unconstitutional. It went further, however, and implied that the Union could be dissolved should other states follow this course.

As Southern belligerence grew, the situation came more into the national limelight. Early in 1830, Senators Robert Hayne and Daniel Webster engaged in a historic debate over the question of nullification. Americans watched with increasing interest as Jackson more fully revealed his own feelings at an important banquet in April, 1830. "Our Union, it must be preserved!" he said, when called upon for a toast. Calhoun, who had never learned the value of brevity, responded with "The Union, next to our liberty most dear! May we always remember that it can only be preserved by respecting the rights of the states and distributing equally the benefits and burdens of the Union!" The exchange did not generate much resentment in South Carolina, but the nullifiers now knew that Jackson was not in their camp.

The event that triggered an expected explosion occurred during the summer of 1831. Two Charleston merchants decided to test the constitutionality of federal tariff laws by refusing to pay certain duties. The local United States district attorney, a sympathizer, refused to prosecute them and promptly lost his job. Jackson said flatly that a state could not nullify a federal law, and he refused to appoint to the vacant position a successor who did not agree with him. Calhoun now came forward openly as South Carolina's defender, issuing a restatement of his *Exposition* and taking his stand against the administration. A head-on collision between Jackson and the Calhoun men was now inevitable.

During 1832, Jackson tried adjusting differences by supporting a revised tariff bill, but the result was a tariff regarded by Southerners as far too protective. South Carolinians especially were not to be silenced, and in November, 1832, at a convention called by the state legislature, an Ordinance of Nullification was passed. It declared that the tariff laws of 1828 and 1832 were unconstitutional, and therefore null and void. February 1, 1833, was fixed as the date when the ordinance was to become effective. The framers of the document made it clear that any attempted coercion on the part of the federal government would result in South Carolina's departure from the Union. They also forbade appeal to the Supreme Court

*A Northern view of South Carolina's ordinance to nullify tariffs forecasts treason, civil war, deception, and finally John Calhoun as a despot.*

*Nicholas Biddle, president of the Bank of the United States, was a victim of Jackson's enmity.*

of any case involving the legality of the nullification.

Jackson was not without an answer. Even as the nullifiers were preparing to meet, the President had spoken his mind to a South Carolina legislator who was about to leave for home. "Tell them," he said, "that they can talk and write resolutions and print threats to their hearts' content. But if one drop of blood be shed there in defiance of the laws of the United States, I will hang the first man of them I can get my hands on, to the first tree I can find." One of South Carolina's Senators told Senator Thomas Hart Benton of Missouri that he doubted if Jackson would go that far. Benton, who had once dueled with the rugged Tennes-

seean, replied, "When Jackson begins to talk about hanging, they can begin to look for the ropes."

There were no hangings. Although Jackson had no compunctions about hanging a man if he thought it necessary, he did not want to antagonize South Carolina so much that other Southern states would join in open opposition to the federal government. Early in 1833, Congress passed Henry Clay's compromise tariff, sharply scaling down the duties. As a face-saver, Congress also passed the Force Bill, which authorized the President to use the armed forces to collect duties if judicial processes were obstructed. The South Carolina convention was now reassembled, and it repealed the Ordinance of Nullification. Then, to save its own face, it declared the Force Bill null and void. Thus both sides left the field of battle chanting victory. The Carolinians actually came off better, for they proved that a state could defy the federal government and obtain a change in national policy. Jackson was gloomy about the whole affair, feeling that secession would be tried again, perhaps over some other issue. "The next pretext will be the Negro or slavery question," he predicted.

### The bank war

During 1832, as the nullification question mounted to a climax, a second front was opened in the political war against Jackson. It was election year, one in which his followers or-

*The prosperous Second Bank of the United States, in Philadelphia, was the cause of the conflict between Biddle and Jackson, who wanted no national bank.*

ganized themselves as the Democratic Party, held a national convention, and nominated their man by the delegates' vote. Anti-Jackson men took the name National Republican Party (soon to be changed to Whig) and chose Henry Clay as their candidate.

Into the Presidential campaign was thrown an issue that Jackson's opponents thought would end his political reign. Henry Clay now persuaded Nicholas Biddle, president of the Second Bank of the United States, to apply for a recharter of that institution in the hope that Jackson's known opposition to the bank would help to defeat him at the polls.

The Second B.U.S., as it was called, had been chartered for a period of 20 years in 1816. After 1823, Biddle, a Philadelphian and a man of letters, was its president. He was opposed by the Jackson men, who were not above attacking his institution on the ground that it was a financial octopus used against the President politically. Jackson himself, in his first annual message to Congress, questioned both the constitutionality of the bank and its ability to establish a uniform and sound currency. The Supreme Court already had ruled upon the first point; on the second, Jackson was decidedly unfair. But this did not detract from the public popularity of his stand.

Despite the nullification question and Henry Clay's carefully contrived bank issue, Jackson won a second

401

*Jackson attacks the many-headed bank hydra with his veto stick. The largest head is Biddle; the others represent the directors of the state branches.*

great victory at the polls in 1832. With it, he carried Van Buren into the Vice-Presidency and further strengthened the New Yorker's claim as Jackson's successor. Among the losers was Nicholas Biddle. Tough-minded Old Hickory now demonstrated his lack of sympathy for known enemies by removing federal deposits of between $10,000,000 and $12,000,000 from the Second B.U.S. several years before its charter expired. He scattered this financial largesse around among some selected state banks that promptly were referred to as "pet banks." Although the action caused a serious dislocation in financial circles, and destroyed an organization that was not to be replaced until the establishment of the Federal Reserve System 75 years later, Jackson had his way.

### Jacksonian diplomacy

In the field of foreign affairs, Jackson was as direct and forthright as ever. In his first inaugural address, the hero of New Orleans and subjugator of the British was as mild as a lamb, promising to preserve international peace and to cultivate friendship to the best of his ability. The world could not argue with his purpose "to ask nothing that is not clearly right and to submit to nothing that is wrong." Jackson, however, was a man rather easily offended, and his interpretation of when he was wronged did not always coincide with that of the other party.

One of the first diplomatic questions to come up in his administration concerned Great Britain. From the days of the Revolution, the Americans had looked longingly at the West Indian trade, from which they were excluded since leaving the Empire. In

The rejected Minister,
We never can make him President,
without first making him Vice-president.
vide webb.

*After Van Buren's rejection by the Senate as minister to England, his enemies sharply mocked Jackson's effort to carry him along to the White House.*

403

*Jackson's strong-arm demand for payment from France's King Louis Philippe for losses suffered during the Napoleonic Wars is lampooned in this print.*

1822, Britain had opened the door a crack, charging American goods heavy duties and still forbidding some articles. After bickering between the two countries, during the Adams administration, Britain again stopped the trade. Jackson now took hold of the knotty problem, politely asking on the one hand for a renewal and on the other threatening nonintercourse between the United States and Canada. The bluff worked. By 1830, he had what he wanted; ships again plied the waters between the British West Indies and the American coast.

With France, he was more violent. American businessmen had claims against the French government dating back to the spoliations of commerce in the Napoleonic days, but had not been able to get a settlement. The Revolution of 1830, which brought Louis Philippe to the throne, gave Jackson a fresh opportunity to press his claims. During the following summer, a treaty was made whereby France promised to pay 25,000,000 francs in six installments.

The spirit of friendship with which the treaty was signed cooled considerably when the French missed their first payment. For a year or so, the American government continued to request payment from the French. Then Jackson recommended reprisals on French property, commenting, "I know the French—they won't pay unless they're made to." The debtors were now highly incensed and vowed that not a sou would be paid until Jackson apologized. He was reported to have roared, "Apologize! I'd see the whole race roasting in hell first!" The French minister, Alphonse Pageot, took his wife, who was the daughter of Major William B. Lewis of the kitchen cabinet, and his son, Andrew Jackson Pageot, back to France. The diplomatic impasse seemed complete.

While Jackson fumed and the French pouted, Great Britain stepped in with an offer to arbitrate. In February, 1836, after Jackson had made a left-handed apology, and the reluctant French were brought around, the offer was accepted. The position of the British arose more out of expediency than generosity, for they did not want to see their ally, France, involved in a needless war with the United States. By early May, Jackson blandly told his countrymen that the diplomatic victory was his: The arrearage had been paid up—and paid with interest.

To a good many Americans of his day, Andrew Jackson was an enigma. On the surface he appeared to be a typically direct and open-mannered Westerner, understanding and easily understood. But beneath this apparent simplicity swirled emotional eddies and crosscurrents that made him sometimes unpredictable. He had studied law, but he had not developed a judicial mind. His actions were more likely to be emotional and unrestrained than thoughtful and controlled. His facility with the English language was remarkable, considering the limitations of his background, and he was to produce some of the ablest state papers of his time. He has no counterpart in European history, and it would be hard to find his parallel

*The Peggy O'Neale Eaton affair is gibed at in this 1834 drawing, with the former barmaid shown dancing before Jackson and his mostly unreceptive cabinet.*

in the history of the United States.

One of Jackson's most impressive qualities was a recognition of his own limitations. Knowing that he was pugnacious and quick-tempered, he deliberately chose for his kitchen cabinet men who counterbalanced some of his weaknesses. This was not always enough, as is revealed by some of his feuds. His conduct in the Eaton-Calhoun battle revealed him as narrow and vindictive—traits that grew more pronounced the longer he stayed in office. After the election triumph of 1832, his demands for adulation and agreement became even greater.

As President he knew exactly what he wanted, as a single sentence from his writings indicates: "The Federal Constitution must be obeyed, states' rights preserved, our national debt must be paid, direct taxes and loans avoided, and the Federal Union preserved." His simple, direct manner appealed greatly to a politically unsophisticated people. They were to discover, as he did, that the realization of these plain-spoken aims was often a good deal more difficult than their mere enunciation.

Jackson's greatest success came not so much from the formulation of any political theory as from his remarkable ability to judge the desires of the people and to translate them into a policy easily understood by the average man. Instinctively, he seemed to plumb people's minds and to know what they wanted. When he came forth with policies shaped to these desires,

he was, of course, enormously popular. Thus, instead of commanding his followers, he simply led them in the direction they wanted to go.

The changes wrought by the Jacksonians were far broader, however, than the simple intentions expressed by the President himself. These men took a somewhat more practical view of democracy than their predecessors, the Jeffersonians, emphasizing economic equality to a generation that, having achieved something of political equality, was now concerning itself with the inequities associated with rising industrialism. Men of Jackson's day had fewer objections to government interference that would insure the workers a fair share of their toil. The common man now demanded an economic as well as a political democracy. The Jacksonians approved the workingmen's struggle for a shorter workday, favored greater guarantees of political rights for the workers, and advocated a more liberal land policy.

Historians have rather heatedly debated whether Jackson was representative of the frontier or of the rising working class in the Northeast. Each side has a good set of arguments, but the likelihood is that Jackson represented Americans as a whole, for the nation was still, to a large extent, a kind of frontier, with all the characteristics of equalitarianism attributed to a frontier society. Old Hickory, in sensing the temper of the times and living up to it, made his era known to later generations as the Age of Jackson.

NEW YORK PUBLIC LIBRARY

# NEW ROADS— THE WATERWAYS

The Louisiana Purchase of 1803 opened the land beyond the Mississippi to the frontier-loving American. The trail breakers had hewed their way into the wilderness on foot and horseback. The homesteaders who followed in their tracks were heading West to stay—they brought families, livestock, tools, seeds for the first sowing. In the early 19th century, before the railroad, the pioneer could go West two ways—by wagon and by boat. The roads of those days were few and bad. Before the coming of the steamboat, travelers were carried slowly along rivers by bargelike flatboats and keelboats. Sometimes a family that reached its new homesite aboard a flatboat used the lumber from it to build its first frontier cabin. In the 1820s, the great steamboat days on the Ohio, Mississippi, and Missouri Rivers began, overcoming the transportation obstacle and hastening the settling of the West.

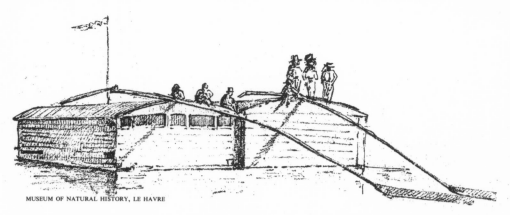

This type of slow, heavy flatboat carried many homesteading families West. These boats were poled along or allowed to drift with the current of the river.

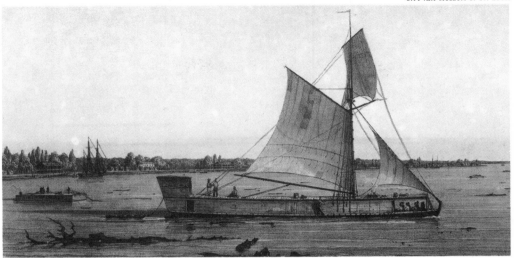

NEW ROADS—THE WATERWAYS

# EARLY RIVER BOATS

Keelboats like the one above were more maneuverable and faster than flatboats and could be sailed on some rivers. The fur traders of the Missouri River country often traveled on the keelboats. They loaded them with supplies for the trip upriver, and if trapping was good, they returned downriver with a load of pelts.

The Mississippi River plantation of 1800, at the left, depended on keelboats and flatboats to send cotton to market and to bring in supplies. The keelboat in mid-river has a cargo of cotton bales. A flatboat (far left) is unloading supplies. The keelboat with the striped canopy in the foreground is a pleasure craft.

409

# HEADING WEST

The keelboat *Philanthropist* (sketched in 1825 by Charles Lesueur, who also drew the scenes opposite) heads down the Ohio. George Caleb Bingham painted Mississippi rivermen (below) playing cards as they drift along.

Cooking on flatboats had to be done over an open fire—one of the hazards of early river-boat travel. The "dining room," lined with bunks, on a passenger-carrying keelboat (below) was uncomfortably primitive.

411

NEW ROADS—THE WATERWAYS

# THE COMING OF STEAM

When this water color was painted by Felix Achille Saint-Aulaire in 1821, on the banks of the Ohio, the steamboat (right) was just beginning to appear on America's great Western rivers. The slow-moving flatboats (left) and keelboats (center), long the only water transportation to the West, ultimately would give way to the faster craft.

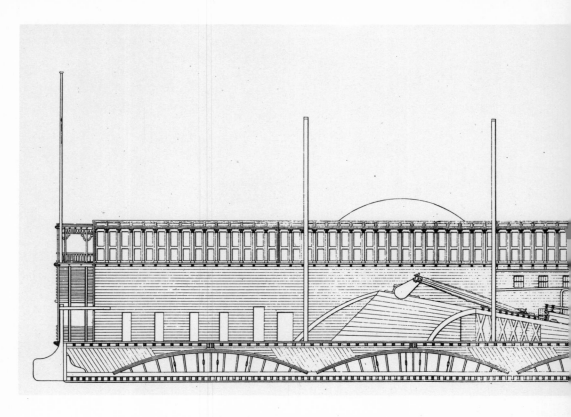

NEW ROADS—THE WATERWAYS

# QUEENS OF THE RIVER

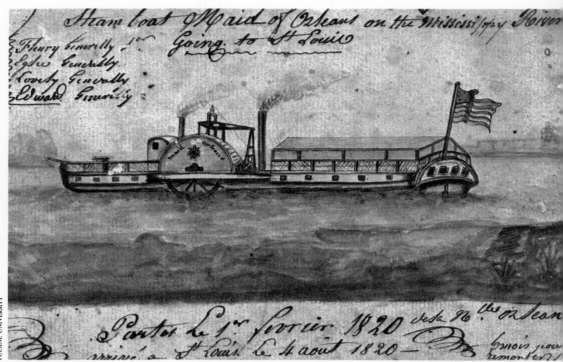

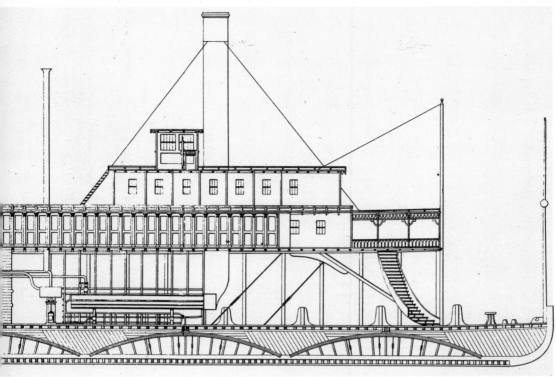

BOTH: *Transactions of the Institution of Naval Architects, 1861*

As more steamboats were built to meet the growing demand, a basic style that was used throughout the steamboat era was developed. The designer's drawing above shows a typical sidewheeler of 1861, which carried both cargo and passengers.

The drawing (right) is a cross-section of the bow of a typical Mississippi steamboat of the 1860s. Because its superstructure was always much wider than its shallow hull, the complicated system of struts and braces shown here was necessary.

This 1820 water color (opposite) of the *Maid of Orleans* is the earliest known picture of a Mississippi steamboat. Although the *Maid* was smaller and less elaborate than the boat diagramed above, she was built from a similar design.

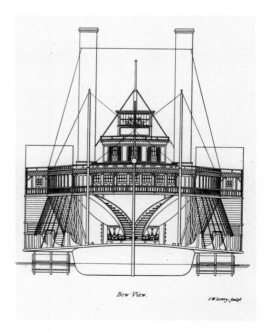

Bow View.

J.W.Lowry, sculpt.

# STEAMBOATS EVERYWHERE

Pittsburgh in 1840 (above), rightly called the Gateway to the West, was a great inland port. A steady flow of homesteaders boarded the steamboats that lined the city's bustling docks. They began their journey by traveling down the Ohio River.

The steamboat, in the scene at the right, is carrying settlers and trappers on the treacherous, snag-ridden upper Missouri River, into the wilderness. A Swiss artist, Carl Bodmer, did the painting in 1833, while making the river journey.

In 1838, when this scene of life on the Mississippi (left) was painted, flatboats were coexisting, because they were cheap, with the ever-expanding fleet of steamboats on the river. Here the flatboatmen are passing the port of Cairo, Illinois.

417

STEAM BOAT *Metamora* ~ NEW YORK AND ALBANY STEAM BOAT PASSENGER LINE

NEW ROADS—THE WATERWAYS

# ALBANY TO NEW YORK

The great days of steamboating were not confined to the Western rivers. The Hudson River steamer *Metamora*, launched in 1846, sailed on the popular Albany-New York run.

# THE CANALS

The canal boat as well as the steamboat played an important role in America's westward expansion. The Erie Canal, shown under construction at the left, was to link the Hudson River with Lake Erie.

The Erie Canal was completed in 1825. In the early days of its operation, its boats and barges were pulled by mules walking the towpath, as shown below. The locks are seen in the background.

PENNSYLVANIA RAILROAD

The route of the Pennsylvania Canal went through the Alleghenies. Boats were hoisted up inclines on railway cars (above).

Homesteaders headed for a new life in the West crowd aboard an Erie Canal barge (below) bound for Buffalo and Lake Erie.

# CHAPTER 15

# SINEWS OF A NATION

During the first half of the 19th century there were industrial and commercial stirrings on the American scene that anticipated fundamental changes in national development. From our earliest beginnings we were primarily an agricultural people, but during these years of the middle period manufacturing and transportation took firm root, foreshadowing a day when the honest plowman would no longer be the dominant economic figure. The transition was slow, almost imperceptible at times, but it was steady. After the Civil War the change would be much faster and more apparent.

There were those who early recognized the need for strong industrial sinews, and they tried to nurse along our weak beginnings. Alexander Hamilton, in his *Report on Manufactures* in 1791, attempted to educate his countrymen on the subject. He pointed out that while we were predominantly agricultural and rural, there were advantages to be had from a more indus-

*St. Louis looked like this in the 1850s. The Dred Scott case first came to trial in the white-domed building at the right.*

trialized economy. An increase in local manufacturing would stimulate immigration, provide a larger domestic market for home-grown foodstuffs, and generally strengthen the nation. These desirable goals had long been blocked by difficult obstacles. Skilled labor was scarce; unskilled labor tended to migrate westward onto cheap lands; inadequate transportation facilities could not distribute properly any kind of manufactures. To compound difficulties, the agricultural class was suspicious of the business world and reluctant to vote capital to help those who were regarded as enemies.

Time would alter the situation. In 1790 the population was about 4,000,000, most of it huddled along the seaboard. By 1850 it was approximately 24,000,000, and a great many of these people lived west of the Appalachians, where the demand for transportation to the East was great. Westerners, and even Easterners, now were quicker to accept American-made products than they had been in an earlier day. Before the War of 1812 we were still mostly dependent upon British manufactures. But the

Napoleonic Wars, and the embargo of Jefferson's time, drove a good many New Englanders into manufacturing. After the War of 1812 they demanded, and received, tariff protection. From that point on, locally manufactured items gradually took the place of imported products, and the ultimate success of American production was assured.

Advances in manufacturing were slow at first. Production was carried

*Through the time of Jefferson, the only important source of industrial power other than the water wheel was a windmill like this American one of 1830.*

*In the 1800s, most American roads were primitive trails through valleys
and around nature's obstacles, like this one painted by Benjamin Latrobe.*

on by the "putting-out" system, in
which rural folks made shoes, spun
yarn, or made cloth out of materials
distributed by local entrepreneurs.
Gradually these workers were gathered
together under a single roof to improve the quality of workmanship and
to eliminate some of the unevenness
of the product. By the '40s, for example, many shoe manufacturers
began to offer a refinement: They
produced right and left shoes, with
some reference to foot sizes. The
new "crooked shoe" was regarded as
quite an improvement over the old
"straights."

In other industries, such as that of
flour milling, there were advances.
As early as the 18th century certain
labor-saving milling methods were
patented, and with the growing demand for wheat products, millers
could offer their customers better
service and an improved product. Yet
distribution was confined to relatively
small sales areas, awaiting a break in
the transportation bottleneck.

Prior to the 1850s, America's industrial world bore little resemblance
to that which we know today. It was
made up of small plants and home
manufactures, and supported by a
local market. A few places assumed a
position of supremacy because of
favorable geography. New England
textile mills, for example, took advantage of water-power sites and
the growing mill towns clustered

425

around them. In the West, Cincinnati's position on the Ohio River (it was also served by canals and rails) gave it such a lead as a meat-packing center that it came to be called Porkopolis. Another "Western" town, Rochester, New York, grew into an important milling center because of its water power and its accessibility to both the Great Lakes and New York City by way of the Erie Canal. Geography also dictated the rise of St. Louis as a commercial capital. Located near the confluence of the Missouri and Mississippi Rivers, it became important at an early date.

Hamilton's prediction that the erection of factories would increase immigration was only partly fulfilled. Cheap land probably accounted for the movement of most people from Europe to America. There were, however, a good many who lingered in the city, unable or unwilling to go on in search of a farmstead. Shortly after the War of 1812 a steady flow of immigrants began to enter the port of New York, a movement that accelerated during the century. Shipping lines did a big business hauling in prospective Americans, not all of whom became farmers. Those with technical skills were encouraged to take jobs in the rising factory system, and they did much to improve the productivity of young industries. Rather than industry encouraging immigration, it was immigration that encouraged industry for a while, because large-scale manufacturing could not have developed without a solid labor base, concentrated at sources of power and transportation. Much later, toward the end of the 19th century, Hamilton's thesis that manufacturing would encourage immigration would be more valid.

### Roots of a factory system

Overshadowed by such national movements as westward expansion or the rise of sectionalism, the growth of American industrial cities was relatively unnoticed during the first half of the 19th century. Yet during these years changes took place very rapidly indeed. One explanation is the alacrity with which Americans accepted mechanization. In England it met opposition because it meant technological unemployment. Here, where there was a labor shortage, machines were welcomed. By 1840 there were some 1,200 cotton factories in this country, most of them in the Northeast. Around them had sprouted factory towns that offered inducements to prospective mill hands.

Not all of our industries grew as rapidly as cotton-textile manufacturing. Our attempts to compete with the English woolen mills had little success before 1860, despite the efforts of Congressmen to provide tariff protection. It was impossible to legislate tastes, and Americans continued to show a preference for English wool.

Nor did the iron industry develop overnight into a full-grown branch of the economy. Textile machinery could be run by water power, but iron foundries needed coal and coke. Our search for a suitable coking coal was a long one, and progress was slow. Pig-iron production grew tenfold during the middle period, but even so, we could boast of only about a half-million tons a year when England was producing 3,000,000 tons annually. The American effort was largely confined to making iron pipes, cast-iron stoves, nails, and other small manufactures. The age of steel would not emerge until after the Civil War. Until then our demands far outran our capacity to refine metals.

During these infant years the fledgling industries tried to develop a sufficient labor force. The problem was greater than one might suppose. Not only were cheap lands drawing off potential mill hands in a land that was characteristically agricultural, but the unsavory reputation of working conditions in the English mills frightened away many who considered employment in our new industries. Mill owners did all they could to make factory work more attractive. New England farm girls were given to understand that life in a textile factory was akin to that of a finishing school. Instruction in the social graces and foreign languages was offered after hours. Parents were promised that the girls would be strictly supervised, both at work and at boarding houses managed by respectable ladies, pref-

*In 1853, Cincinnati, Ohio, was called the Queen City of the West, for then it was still considered Western and was the largest community in its area.*

erably widows with small children. Thousands of young women were induced to accept such employment. It offered them an opportunity to learn a trade and be self-supporting.

The use of women and children in industry, the growth of immigration after 1820, and popular hostility to unions expressed in anticonspiracy laws made it hopeless for labor to try to organize. Employers quickly assumed complete control and called the play at every turn. As early as 1825 nearly all adult males were entitled to vote, and there was thus a possibility of achieving gains at the ballot box. But even here the results were disappointing. The most the workers could hope for was the ideal of the 10-hour day, and even that would not be achieved without a struggle. Collective bargaining through some sort of labor union was just a hazy, dimly visualized theory.

### Horsepower on the highways

Throughout colonial and postcolonial days America's inland transportation was indeed primitive. The original 13 colonies fixed their eyes upon the sea, and thought in terms of international trade. Those who chose to engage in trade between colonies, and later between states, believed that the Atlantic Ocean was the best and cheapest thoroughfare. There was no adequate network of roads linking together the political units that became the United States. Nor did there seem to be much pros-

*By 1850, heavy industry had already begun to specialize, as shown by the Novelty Iron Works in New York, makers of boilers and engines for steamers.*

*Women going to work in an early New England mill in a rustic setting, as painted by Winslow Homer, shows the change from agriculture to manufacturing.*

pect that this deficiency would be soon remedied.

A few rivers, such as the Hudson and the Delaware, were navigable for varying distances, but in the South and in New England the fall line was too close to the sea to make river transport feasible. West of the great Appalachian Range there were possibilities in such broad and important rivers as the Ohio, or along the Great Lakes that stretched out for hundreds of miles. But between the Atlantic seaboard and these waterways lay forbidding mountains. Somehow, they would have to be breached.

For a long time most Americans saw no reason to worry about such matters, for there was little in the West to attract the businessman. Yet the westward movement was continuous, as it would be throughout the 19th century, and as the War of 1812 faded into the past, new thousands found homes beyond the mountains. The new Westerners were eager to trade, and Eastern businessmen began to realize that opportunity did not lie only in the Atlantic Ocean. Just beyond the mountain passes lay timber, pelts, salt, lead, hogs, cattle, and grain. And almost like the Indians, the white Westerners would take New England gewgaws and small manufactures in exchange.

The earliest solution to the problem of land transportation was the turnpike, or improved road. By 1794

429

the Lancaster Turnpike, running from Philadelphia to Lancaster in Pennsylvania, had become the model for hundreds like it. Aside from its crushed-stone surface, which made it an "all-weather" road, its easy 4% grade, and its fine bridges, the road had another distinctive feature: It was privately constructed. This was necessary because neither the state nor the federal government had exhibited much interest in highway building. In the case of the Lancaster Turnpike, built at a cost of $465,000, the state cooperated to the extent of granting the company the authority to condemn the necessary right-of-way. Then, after setting up toll gates seven miles apart along the road, the managers charged for the passage of people, animals, and vehicles, the last being assessed according to the width of their wheels. The Lancaster experiment was not a great success from a financial standpoint, but the idea appealed to Americans so much that by the time Albert Gallatin made his report on roads in 1808, he could write that in the state of New York alone there were 67 such companies, which were managing 900 miles of privately constructed road.

Impatiently the Westerners waited, vexed at conservative Eastern financiers, whose own roads were relatively good, and who were reluctant to invest their money in projects that might encourage westward migration and thereby increase the labor shortage in the Northeast. Pennsylvania, across whose territory many pioneers would have to travel, was at last moved to buy $100,000 worth of stock in a company that promised to extend the Lancaster Turnpike westward to Wheeling, on the Ohio River. This extension, the Cumberland (or National) Road was built at a cost of about $13,000 a mile, and after many difficulties, both legal and technical, it was finally completed in 1818. Ohioans showed their interest in the project by turning over a percentage of the sales from public lands in the new state to secure a connection with the Atlantic Ocean. Happy, too, were the merchants of Baltimore and Philadelphia, who hoped that their respective cities would now emerge as the commercial leaders of the seaboard.

The Cumberland Road was warmly

*In 1821, even in winter, stages went from Providence to Worcester in a day, for $3.*

welcomed by those who wished to trade or travel. Over it, and its counterparts that soon sprang up, flowed all kinds of traffic from private carriages to the crudest carts. Newly formed stagecoach lines called by such names as the June Bug Line, the Pioneer Line, and the National Line did a flourishing business. That the new means of travel was not the ultimate in comfort is suggested by the name of the one called the Shake Gut Line. Despite such discomforts, passengers were delighted that they could bump across the land at an average speed of close to six miles an hour and that the Ohio River was now only $17.25 away from Baltimore.

Freighters made equally good use of the Lancaster-Cumberland Road. As early as 1817, a year before the road to Wheeling was finished, one contemporary wrote that 12,000 wagons had arrived at Pittsburgh from Baltimore and Philadelphia. The highway made possible a new kind of triangular trade by which enterprising merchants could send selected goods overland to the headwaters of the Ohio, raft them down as far as New Orleans or sell them along the way, and then proceed by ship back to the East Coast to start the process all over again.

New equipment matched the new roads. The Conestoga wagon soon became the most famous freight vehicle on the turnpike. Its boatlike shape, with each end about a foot higher than the middle to make it more maneuverable on rough terrain, made it unique. Topped with canvas supported by huge bows, it was the

*A crowd watches as this stagecoach, pulled by 10 horses and called the Seventy Six, leaves with its overflow of three passengers seated on the top.*

prototype of the prairie schooner soon to be so widely known west of the Missouri River. These broad-wheeled wagons, pulled by six-horse teams, carried enormous loads.

In addition to their contribution to transportation, the Conestoga wagons left a social note on the American scene. The drivers, a tough, rough-housing breed, found that along with profanity one of the necessities of their calling was a good cigar. They complained so about the high price of cigars that an enterprising individual devised a smaller, but cheaper and more potent, product. They were so widely used by the teamsters that they became known as Conestogies, later shortened to "stogies."

One of the most notable results of such improved transportation facil-

ities to the west side of the mountains was the decline in freight rates. In 1817 it cost $9.50 to ship 100 pounds of freight from Pittsburgh to Philadelphia. Within a year that cost fell to $6.50. But rates were still high for bulkier products. The charge of $13 a barrel for hauling flour over the same distance kept the volume low for some time to come. While the turnpike was a satisfactory solution to the problem of passenger and small-freight haulage, another answer had to be found for heavier and larger items. The solution was the canal.

### Nautical teamsters

As merchants and freighters contemplated ways of hauling great quantities, they rediscovered a fact known for centuries: Water transpor-

tation was the cheapest. It was esti-
mated that four horses could pull a
ton 12 miles a day over an ordinary
road and 18 miles over a good turnpike, but they could haul 100 tons 24
miles by water in the same period.
Canals—man-made waterways—were
an ancient conception. They appeared
to be the answer to interior America's
growing transportation needs.

The attraction to canals was more
than taproom talk. City people around
the fine harbor of New York regarded
them with a sense of urgency. By 1818
Baltimore and Philadelphia, now con-
nected to the Ohio River by turnpike, threatened to eclipse New York
as a commercial center. Already the
steamboat was becoming a practi-
cality on Western waters. Steam would
make a two-way street out of the

*A pageant was held when the first boat
through the Erie Canal reached New York
in 1825. The canal created a water route
from Lake Erie to the Hudson River.*

Mississippi-Ohio River system, and
then the road eastward from Pittsburgh would be clogged with an even
greater traffic. Provincial as well as
metropolitan New Yorkers, who had
assumed a take-it-or-leave-it attitude
about the West, now awoke to the
facts of economic life, and soon they
embarked upon a crash program of
canal building.

By 1817 the New York legislature
was persuaded to pass legislation that
made possible construction of the
Erie Canal. Paced by the enthusiasm
of New York Governor DeWitt Clin-
ton, and under the direction of two
lawyers who practiced engineering on

*There was a canal through Virginia's Dismal Swamp by 1805, with lumber its main commodity, but the artist imagined the kind of craft that traveled it.*

the side, the amateur canal builders went to work. In what turned out to be a school for canal engineers, the project was completed with remarkable speed, considering that it was done largely by hand and by horse. In 1825 the canal's 363 miles between Buffalo and Albany were opened to traffic. A contemporary writer observed, "They have built the longest canal in the world in the least time, with the least experience, for the least money, and to the greatest public benefit." Within 25 years the writer

might have added another significant fact: In that short time the canal's tolls paid for its construction several times over.

Long before that, other Americans had seen the tremendous possibilities of canals. Once a connection between the Atlantic Ocean and the Great Lakes was assured, Midwestern promoters began to build a whole network of canals between those inland oceans and the Ohio River. Now farmers from New York to Illinois watched teams of stocky horses plod-

434

ding canal towpaths, tugging along a new breed of sailors and their cargoes. While canal transportation was designed primarily to haul heavy freight, it was widely used by passengers. On the Erie Canal, packet boats moved along at four miles an hour, charging fares of 3¢ to 4¢ a mile, for which passengers received not only bed and board, but a degree of comfort denied by closely packed stagecoaches.

The freshly cut ditches and the brightly colored boats that glided along them meant a great deal to inland communities. Not only could the necessaries of life be brought in more cheaply, but for the first time it was feasible to ship out large quantities of agricultural produce. The effect was dual: Western farmers could get away from their homespun industries to a degree that permitted them to specialize agriculturally and to deal in a cash economy; and further, rising New England manufacturing centers could both find a market for their wares and rely upon a supply of Western farm products for their tables.

Advanced transportation facilities, while important to the nation at large, were particularly welcomed by the various sections. Westerners watched with delight as falling freight rates drove down the price of goods brought in, and at the same time gave them a greater share of the profits when they sold their produce. Real-estate and personal-property values in Ohio rose much faster in counties having canals than in those not served by them.

Western cities grew rapidly, thanks to these improvements. Cleveland, for example, saw its population grow fiftyfold in the second quarter of the 19th century. Toledo, Chicago, Milwaukee, and Detroit also experienced boom times as immigrants poured in, eager to find farms.

In the Northeast, the effect of Western agricultural competition brought about specialization in dairy and truck farming to take advantage of nearby expanding markets in the growing Eastern cities. From a long-range point of view, the canals thus provided an important economic link connecting interdependent regions, the Northeast and the Midwest. Also, the specialization now made possible in each section tended to break down antagonisms Westerners had harbored against their Eastern brethren for decades. As the American Civil War approached, this became more and more important.

### The age of steam

Canals solved some of the problems of transporting freight that turnpikes could not, but they were by no means the final answer. Aside from being expensive to build, and in rough country nearly impossible to construct, they were often frozen into uselessness during the winter months. When the canals were thus closed, and roads made impassable by long stretches of bad weather, huge amounts of produce would pile up in warehouses to await the coming of

435

spring. To carry heavy freight long distances at relatively low rates and in all kinds of weather, transportation men turned to a new instrument—the railroad.

Considering American ingenuity and the great need for transportation facilities, it is surprising that the railroad was not developed earlier. Its essential elements were well known before 1800 in England, where stationary steam engines were used to haul coal cars out of the mines. Yet even the Eastern regions of the United States, with available money and a traffic potential, did little in railroading before the 1830s. They probably would have delayed even longer had not the whip of necessity lashed them into action. New England glumly watched New York reap huge rewards from the Erie Canal. The Pennsylvanians tried to duplicate the feat by building enormously expensive canal systems. Southerners looked on, jealous of the busy Northerners but thwarted by the great mountains that reared up to confound even prospective canal builders. The railroad—new-fangled, dangerous and possibly impractical—appeared to be a risky but necessary venture.

During 1830 and 1831 the legislature of Massachusetts chartered three railroads. All of them were completed in five years and all of them, of course,

radiated from Boston. By 1842 rail connections between Boston and Albany, on the Erie Canal, were completed, with the aid of funds from nervous New England capitalists and almost $4,000,000 from the state of Massachusetts. Between 1830 and 1850 almost 3,000 miles of railroad were constructed in New England. By the end of that period Yankee manufactures were being carried all the way to the Great Lakes by rail. Indirectly, DeWitt Clinton may be credited for loosening a number of tightly strung Puritan purses. It was bet or get out of the game.

The South accepted the railroad much more readily but for the same reason—fear of commercial rivals. In South Carolina the city fathers of Charleston watched anxiously as New Orleans and even Savannah prospered. In 1828 Charleston's Chamber of Commerce secured a charter for a railroad to run from that city to Hamburg, on the Savannah River opposite Augusta, Georgia. The road, 136 miles in length, was projected for the purpose of capturing some of Savannah's trade. When it was completed, in 1833, it was the world's longest railroad. By no means satisfied, the

*This 1830 locomotive, the second made in the United States, ran between Charleston and Harrisburg. On this trip it carried a band to entertain its few passengers.*

Carolinians dreamed of the day they could tap the Ohio River by rail and become a great international trading center, exporting Midwestern cereals and livestock. Neighboring Georgians saw the point, and decided to build west to capture frontier traffic. They constructed the Western & Atlantic, which was state owned and operated. It was 1851 before this road reached Chattanooga and finally Memphis, but despite many delays it still was the first to tap the South's western back country.

The early railroads were crude and certainly dangerous contraptions. So feeble were the power units that occasionally a horse was carried along as a "spare" in case of difficulties. Some roads stored their locomotives during the winter and used horses, to insure service. The track, timbers laid end to end and covered with narrow straps of thin metal, varied in gauge

part of those who had invested heavily in canal bonds, and of farmers and tavern operators who made money by feeding stagecoach horses and passengers along the turnpikes. These vested interests were not without influence. In 1833, when the Utica & Schenectady Railroad applied for a charter, the New York legislature stipulated that nothing but passengers and baggage could be carried by rail. Later the legislators relented and allowed the carriage of freight, provided the railroad paid the state canal fund the amount of money it would have collected in fees had the goods gone by canal boat. Such opposition was gradually overcome by the demonstrated superiority of the railroad and the public's enthusiastic reception of it.

In the West, much of which was not served by either canals or improved highways, there was no prejudice against the rail lines, but they suffered from other limitations. The new land was characterized by a sparse and widely spread population, an absence of large cities, chronic lack of capital, and a traditional animosity toward the Eastern investing class that might be induced to sink money into rail

from four to six feet. On these primitive roads one might find a half-dozen different gauges in the same region, a condition that prevented through lines from developing. Signal systems were in their infancy, and through their failure, or the tendency of the strap-iron rails to come loose and knife through coach floors, a number of bad accidents occurred.

Atop all these problems lay a great hostility toward the railroads on the ventures. Nevertheless, the railroad was the answer to the West's problems, and despite all these difficulties the new form of transportation came to that region.

The task of penetrating the great Appalachian Range with rail lines was accomplished largely during the late 1840s and early 1850s. In view of the existing engineering knowledge and the available facilities, the feat in many respects was more significant than the achievements of those who later crossed the Sierras and Rockies with their construction crews. The New York & Erie reached the Great Lakes by 1851, the same year the Western & Atlantic entered Chattanooga. The Baltimore & Ohio was completed in 1852, and within another year the New York Central road was organized.

After some organizational fumbling, and experiments in state construction, railroad building was entrusted to the hands of private enterprise. Flinty-eyed entrepreneurs made the most of their opportunities. However, they did not do it without help. Rather early the roads became the accepted carriers of mail and troops, and the subsidies granted them lent much-needed financial support. Far more important aid came from government grants of land. When, in 1850, the Illinois Central was given alternate sections of land on each side of its route, a practice was established that later would make possible the construction of transcontinental lines.

Before the time of the Civil War the government had handed out about 32,000,000 acres for this purpose.

### Empire builders on rails

The turnpikes, canals, and railroads together supplied the essential transportation links for the development of American manufacture and commerce. Of the three, the railroad came to be the most important because of its efficiency and greater adaptability. Its advantages over the turnpike were obvious, and it could penetrate new country inaccessible to canals, a factor that after 1860 overcame the waterways.

New states were not long in taking advantage of the cheaper means of travel. As early as 1845 the Michigan state legislature provided funds to pay an agent, stationed in New York, for sending on any immigrants he could find. That state also published thousands of pamphlets for distribution throughout Europe, hoping to attract land-hungry farmers. Neighboring Wisconsin followed a similar course, fearful that its opportunities might go unnoticed. When Illinois failed to join the competition, the Illinois Central Railroad took up the cause and embarked upon the greatest advertising campaign of that day. Its pamphlets were sent to thousands of post offices, with requests to tack them up on a convenient wall. Railroad advertising appeared in all Eastern port-city newspapers and in those of every little agricultural community sus-

# ILLINOIS CENTRAL RAILROAD COMPANY
### OFFER FOR SALE
## ONE MILLION ACRES OF SUPERIOR FARMING LANDS,
### IN FARMS OF
## 40, 80 & 160 acres and upwards at from $8 to $12 per acre.
### THESE LANDS ARE
## NOT SURPASSED BY ANY IN THE WORLD.
### THEY LIE ALONG
## THE WHOLE LINE OF THE CENTRAL ILLINOIS RAILROAD,
For Sale on LONG CREDIT, SHORT CREDIT and for CASH, they are situated near TOWNS, VILLAGES, SCHOOLS and CHURCHES.

*The Illinois Central was the first railroad to use its federal land grants to lure settlers onto its line and out to land that ran along its right of way.*

pected of having discontented farmers. The company was eager to utilize the lands granted it, both for cash profit and to populate its route with prospective customers. In so doing, it set a pattern followed by a majority of the trans-Mississippi roads a few years later.

By the 1850s American growth was a matter of surprised comment, even among Americans. In the West, the fastest-growing part of the nation, it was the railroad that was of prime importance in this development. It helped to populate the new country, particularly its more remote parts.

It provided America with a whole new industry—railroading itself. The business of manufacturing locomotives, cars, rails, and equipment was important to a growing steel industry. The railroad's ability to transport passengers and all kinds of freight rapidly gave older sections, such as New England, new industrial opportunities, while it allowed Western agriculture to specialize as it never had before. Even in its infancy it was predicted that the railroad would become the economic bloodstream of America, a forecast that has abundantly been fulfilled.

**MAIN TEXT CONTINUES IN VOLUME 6**

*It was the cotton kingdom, ruled by landowning whites but based upon the hard labor of the Negro, that Eli Whitney's revolutionary invention brought strongly into existence. This Currier and Ives portrays the legend of charm that was associated with plantation life.*

# Eli Whitney:
# Nemesis of the South

A SPECIAL CONTRIBUTION BY
## ARNOLD WHITRIDGE

*A New England schoolteacher invented the cotton gin that revolutionized the South, and then he laid the foundations for the North's industrial power that would conquer it.*

Any American who ruminates about the origins of the Civil War—and that should mean not only professional historians but everyone in the United States, North and South, who has ever been spellbound by the story of his country—will find himself sooner or later confronted by an ingenious contraption for removing seeds from the cotton boll, known as the cotton gin.

This device, invented by Eli Whitney, a totally unknown young man just out of Yale College, changed the whole pattern of cotton production. No invention ever answered a more pressing need.

Immediately after graduating from Yale in 1792, Whitney was engaged as a private tutor for a family in Georgia. On his way to take up his post, he made the acquaintance of Mrs. Nathanael Greene, widow of the Revolutionary general, who was returning to Savannah after spending the summer in the North. An invitation to stay at Mrs. Greene's plantation, all the more welcome when he discovered that his prospective employer had hired another man in his place, brought him into contact with the cotton aristocracy of the neighborhood. Whitney soon endeared himself to his

hostess by his extraordinary "handiness." There was nothing this big, rambling man with the extraordinary deft fingers could not make or mend.

As a boy on the farm, the oldest of five children, he had always preferred puttering around his father's metalworking shop to doing the farm chores. He was born in Westboro, Massachusetts, in 1765, the year of the Stamp Act. By the time he was grown, the exciting days of the Revolution were over, and the farmers of Massachusetts were learning to their amazement that independence and prosperity did not necessarily go hand in hand. Some of them, discouraged by debts they could not pay, joined Shays' Rebellion against the state government, but Eli Whitney stuck to the farm and eked out the family income by manufacturing nails, even hiring a helper to fill his orders. When the demand for nails slacked off, he turned to making hatpins and walking canes. Neighbors got into the habit of looking up Eli whenever they needed anything repaired. For one of them he even made a violin, which was said to have produced "tolerable good music."

At the age of 18, it came home to him that he needed a college degree if he was ever to be anything more than a clever mechanic. The family was not sympathetic: By the time he had prepared himself for college, he would be too old, and besides, they could not afford it. Eli listened to all their complaints and then disregarded them. He taught school for three winters, finally won his father's consent, and was admitted to Yale in 1789, when he was 23.

*When Whitney was painted in 1822, three years before his death, by Samuel F. B. Morse, he had little idea of the effect of his inventions.*

He was not a brilliant student, but when the Reverend Ezra Stiles, president of Yale, was asked to recommend a suitable person for a private tutor out of the graduating class of 1792, Whitney was the one he chose.

Evidently Mrs. Greene in Savannah had faith in him, too, and when a party of her friends, officers who had served under General Greene in the Revolution, were discussing the deplorable state of agriculture in their neighborhood, she referred them to the young Yale graduate who was staying with her. They were bemoaning the fact that there was no quick, practical way of separating short-staple cotton from its seed. It took a slave 10 hours to separate one pound of lint from three pounds of the small, tough seeds. Under those conditions, no one in the South could afford to grow cotton, and yet in other parts of the world, cotton was becoming a semiprecious commodity. "Gentlemen," said Mrs. Greene, "tell your troubles to Mr. Whitney. He can make anything."

Mr. Whitney could and did. Within two weeks he had produced a model of the cotton gin, an ingenious device that was destined to have an ultimately disastrous effect upon the people it enriched. The cotton was dragged through a wire screen by means of toothed cylinders revolving toward each other. A revolving brush cleaned the cylinders, and the seeds fell into another compartment. A later model, run by water power, could produce 300 to 1,000 pounds a day.

Whitney wrote to his father that he hoped to keep his invention a "profound secret," but word of it spread so quickly that long before he could get to Washington and take out a patent, his workshop had been broken into and his machine examined. The interlopers discovered that the gin was easy to copy, and because it was, cotton was planted on a scale never dreamed of before. In 1792, the United States was exporting only 138,000 pounds. Two years later, that figure had risen to 1,601,000. Never had any invention made such an immediate impression upon society, abroad as well as at home.

In England, the invention of spinning frames and power looms had created a demand that could be filled only from the Southern states. Supplies from the Levant, from Guiana, and from the West Indies, which had met nearly all needs down to 1794, fell into the background as the export of American slave-grown and mechanically ginned cotton suddenly began to climb. By the end of the first quarter of the 19th century, America was shipping to Liverpool more than three-quarters of all the cotton used in the United

Kingdom. Eli Whitney had conjured up an army of 450,000 cotton workers in England. Ten thousand power looms and 240,000 hand looms secured the cotton planters against the danger of a glutted market.

The existence of this market and being able to supply it with ease and profit made cotton planting the greatest industry in the South. The Louisiana Purchase had opened to slave-holding settlement and culture a vast domain of the richest soil on earth in a region peculiarly adapted to the expanding production of cotton. As production grew, so did the value of the Negro. By 1825, when cotton was selling at 15¢ a pound, a good Negro field hand who 20 years earlier had been worth only $500 would often bring $1,500 on a New Orleans auction block.

The phenomenal success of the cotton industry, for which Eli Whitney was directly responsible, gave birth in the South to an entirely new conception of slavery. In the early days of the Republic, the most thoughtful Southerners, including Washington and Jefferson, had deprecated slavery as an evil that must eventually be swept away. No one denied that slavery was morally wrong and a menace to the country. Almost every Virginian hoped to make real the words of his state's bill of rights, "that all men are by nature equally free and independent." As the Marquis de Chastellux, a major general in Rochambeau's army in America during the Revolution, wrote,

"They are constantly talking of abolishing slavery, and of contriving some other means of cultivating their estates."

Such ideas gradually came to be regarded as old-fashioned. What, asked Daniel Webster in 1850, had created the new feeling in favor of slavery in the South, so that it became an institution to be cherished—"no evil, no scourge, but a great religious, social and moral blessing? I suppose this is owing to the rapid growth and sudden extension of the cotton plantations of the South."

The doctrine that cotton was king, and that all other interests in the nation would bow before it, had permeated the whole South by the middle of the century. Few of the Northerners who scoffed at this doctrine remembered that it was a Northern inventor who gave slavery its new lease on life. It was hard to protest against a system upon which the whole prosperity of one section of the country seemed to hinge. Unwittingly, Eli Whitney had set in motion an undercurrent against the notions of equality and freedom. He himself made nothing out of his cotton gin, but he was nonetheless the founder of the cotton empire—an empire that everybody believed would inevitably collapse if the underpinning of slavery were removed.

The cotton gin, like many other inventions, turned out to be so valuable to the world as to be worthless to its inventor. The government could offer Whitney no protection

*Whitney's cotton gin was the most notable of America's early contributions to the Industrial Revolution. This model is one of several made by Whitney in applying for a patent. He filed his first application in 1793 with Thomas Jefferson, who was then Secretary of State and head of the Patent Office, but he never received full protection for his invention.*

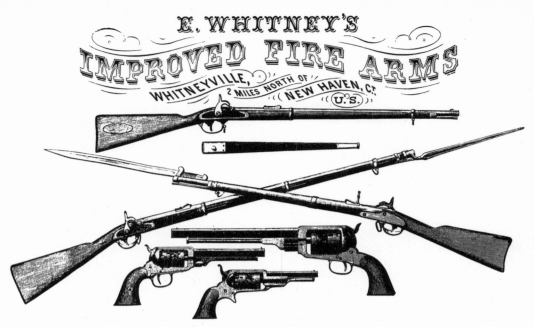

*The reproductions above are from an old advertisement for Whitney's
gun factory, where he filled his first government contract in 1798.*

against the infringement of patent rights. The
suits he brought were tried before juries of
the very men who were breaking the patents.

Unable to make a living out of the cotton
gin, Whitney turned his back on the South.
He settled in New Haven and determined to
devote himself to the production of something
profitable—something that could not easily
be copied and appropriated by others. In
1798, disturbed by the danger of war with
France, he wrote to Oliver Wolcott, Secretary
of the Treasury, offering to manufacture "ten
or fifteen thousand Stand of Arms." By "stand
of arms" was meant the complete arms necessary to equip a soldier—the musket, bayonet,
ramrod, wiper, and screw driver.

After some haggling, the offer was accepted.
Whitney journeyed down to Washington and
returned to New Haven with a contract in his
pocket for 10,000 muskets, selling for $13.40
each, to be delivered within two years. He
proposed to manufacture these muskets on a
new principle—the principle of interchangeable parts.

Here was a man who as early as 1798 could
visualize the government's need of a constant
supply of firearms, who could devise methods
of production that would guarantee such a

supply, and who, handicapped by the lack of
a machine that would enable workmen to cut
metal according to pattern, proceeded to invent one that has remained unchanged in
principle for more than a century and a half.
This milling machine, as it was called, was
the cornerstone of his new system of interchangeable parts. Life in America had produced plenty of mechanics, particularly in
New England, but few craftsmen. What Whitney did was to substitute for the skill of the
craftsman the uniformity of the machine.

Foreigners have often observed as one of
the characteristics of American industry
that we build from the top down rather than
from the ground up. Eli Whitney did not start
with a few workmen and then gradually expand. He tooled up first. Before a single work-
man walked into his factory, he designed and
built all the machinery he would need for his
method of production. At the same time he
proved himself a practical businessman as
well as an inventor. He understood how to
obtain contracts, finance their execution, and
provide funds for future expansion.

The importance of what Whitney was doing
did not readily penetrate the official mind.

His friend Wolcott had been replaced in the Treasury by Samuel Dexter, a Massachusetts lawyer, who instinctively distrusted theories not sanctioned by experience. Whitney's methods seemed to him unorthodox. As if to justify his suspicions, Whitney was soon running behind on his schedule of deliveries. In the first year, only 500 guns were produced instead of the stipulated 4,000.

Fortunately the new President, Thomas Jefferson, was blessed with a receptive, ranging mind. The idea of interchangeable parts was already familiar to him. In 1785, while minister to France, he had visited the workshop of a Monsieur LeBlanc, who was making muskets on exactly that principle. Jefferson himself had put together the parts of 50 locks, "taking pieces at hazard as they came to hand." He was so impressed by this new method of manufacture that he suggested bringing LeBlanc over to America, but the government was not interested in newfangled techniques. Nor indeed was the French government, which probably distrusted any invention that might lead to unemployment.

In England, too, other men had anticipated Whitney. Joseph Bramah, the great machine designer, and Marc Brunel, a young French Royalist officer who had been driven out of his country during the Revolution, had manufactured pulley blocks with interchangeable parts for the British navy, but it was left to an American to apply the process to mass production and put it to the service of mankind.

Whitney himself probably never realized how far his system would reach. The new technique that had been used for the manufacture of firearms was soon found to be no less applicable to other industries. The Connecticut clockmakers began making brass clocks instead of wooden clocks, as soon as the advantages of interchangeable parts were recognized. Elias Howe and Isaac Singer followed with the sewing machine, and before the outbreak of the Civil War, Cyrus McCormick and his rivals were producing the harvesters and reapers that rolled back the frontier and revolutionized farming the world over.

For these inventions and a hundred others,
Eli Whitney paved the way. The successful application of his theory proved a landmark in the over-all growth of American mass production. In Europe, however, where there was no shortage of skilled labor, the idea made slow progress. It caught on only in gunmaking, where the advantages were too obvious to be ignored. By the middle of the 19th century, nearly every government in Europe was supplied with American gunmaking machinery.

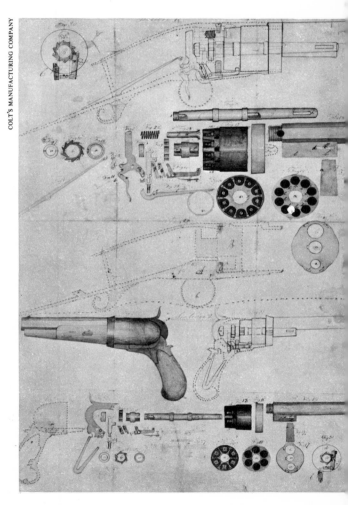

*The system of interchangeable parts, devised by Whitney and carried on by Samuel Colt in Whitney's armory, is shown in this 1853 illustration of Colt's first patent for his firearms.*

447

In the Southern states, the planters who had profited so enormously from the cotton gin paid no attention to the increasing tempo of industrial activity in the North. South Carolina paid $50,000 to Whitney as a belated acknowledgment of what society owed him, but no one in the South seemed aware of the new techniques in manufacture that he evolved—techniques of which the seceding states were soon to find themselves desperately in need. Conditions of labor, soil, and climate had produced a static society that refused to accept the implications of the 19th century.

It is one of the ironies of history that the man who inadvertently contributed to the downfall of the South by his invention of the cotton gin should also have blazed the trail leading to the technological supremacy of the North. The loss of the will to fight in the closing days of the Confederacy can be traced in large part to the feeling that the South had reached the limit of its resources, whereas in the North every deficiency in equipment could always be made good.

No distinction can be made between the Union and the Confederate soldier in their inherent fighting ability, but in the quantity as well as the quality of their equipment the advantage was all with the Northerner. Although the extraordinarily resourceful General Josiah Gorgas, Confederate chief of ordnance, managed to keep his armies supplied with the necessary weapons and munitions up to the very end of the war, even he could not keep pace with the inventiveness and the productivity of Northern arsenals and factories. More than once, a single Union regiment, armed with breech-loading rifles, held in check a whole brigade armed with the ordinary musket. As one Confederate soldier put it, "It's no use for us to fight you'uns with that kind of gun."

The disparity in clothing and equipment was even more marked than the disparity in weapons. The Southern soldier had to find most of his own equipment, whereas the Northerner was supplied by the government. If the Union soldier faced privation, as he often did, it was the fault of shady contractors and incompetent quartermasters. The New England factories were turning out all the uniforms, the boots, and the varied accouterments he could possibly need.

The Civil War was the first of the truly modern wars, in which the industrial potential of a nation forms the foundation on which all military plans and achievements must ultimately be built. Given that situation, the advantage was all with the North.

Before the war even began, William Tecumseh Sherman warned a Southern friend that a purely agricultural nation like the South could not hope to win against a nation of mechanics. "You are bound to fail," he said, and events bore him out. As the war went on, the entire Southern economy came under intolerable strain. In the end, it simply became impossible for the Confederacy to carry the burden any longer.

On the other hand, the North could produce, in almost any required volume, the infinite variety and number of goods needed to support a nation at war. For this technique it was, to a large extent, indebted to Eli Whitney.

Whitney died in 1825, long before the "irrepressible conflict" had cast its shadow over American history. He himself was unaware of the part he had played in the expansion of slavery, just as he was unaware of the mighty industrial forces he had set in motion. He had invented the cotton gin and he had manufactured muskets on a new system for a war against France that never materialized, but by those two achievements he had affected the whole course of American history. By the first he riveted slavery on the South and thus created a tension between the two sections of the country that could be resolved only by war. And by the second he gave an impetus to the mass production of inexpensive goods that has created what the world knows as the American standard of living, and that has reunited us, with all the differences in our backgrounds, into an amazingly homogeneous nation.

*Arnold Whitridge has been Master of Calhoun College, Yale University, and professor in the Department of History, Arts, and Letters. His most recent book is* No Compromise! *(1960).*

# FOR FURTHER READING

Adams, James T. *The Adams Family.* Boston: Little, Brown, 1930. The chapter on the sixth President is excellent.

Adams, John Quincy. *Diary,* ed. Allan Nevins. New York: Scribner, 1951. An unusual personality and major political figure, as reflected in his diary.

Babcock, Kendrick Charles. *Rise of American Nationality, 1811–1819.* New York: Harpers, 1906. Discusses the formation of a national consciousness.

Beveridge, Albert J. *The Life of John Marshall.* 4 volumes. Boston: Houghton Mifflin, 1916–19. A biography of Marshall and a fine history of the period.

Brooks, Van Wyck. *The World of Washington Irving.* New York: E. P. Dutton, 1944. Portrays American arts, letters, and life from 1800–40.

Corwin, Edward S. *John Marshall and the Constitution.* New Haven: Yale University Press, 1921. A commentary on the Supreme Court's role in the early 19th century.

Curti, Merle. *The Growth of American Thought.* New York: Harpers, 1943. A one-volume statement of the changes that have occurred in American thought.

Dangerfield, George. *The Era of Good Feelings.* New York: Harcourt, Brace, 1952. The term usually applied to James Monroe's Presidency is extended to include the administration of John Quincy Adams.

De Tocqueville, Alexis. *Democracy in America.* 2 volumes. New York: Vintage Books (paperback), 1954. One of the classic studies of American democracy, published in 1835 by a Frenchman and still relevant today.

Hulbert, Archer Butler. *The Paths of Inland Commerce.* New Haven: Yale University Press, 1920. A brief but effective study of the development of transportation.

Kirkland, Edward C. *A History of American Economic Life.* New York: F. S. Crofts, 1932. Still one of the standard works of American economic history.

Mesick, Jane L. *The English Traveller in America, 1785–1835.* New York: Columbia University Press, 1922. A collection of the accounts of those who traveled the early roads.

Perkins, Dexter. *Hands Off: A History of the Monroe Doctrine.* Boston: Little, Brown, 1941. The best summary of recent historical scholarship on the famous document.

Schlesinger, Arthur M., Jr. *The Age of Jackson.* Boston: Little, Brown, 1945. One of the major interpretations of the Jackson era.

Syrett, Harold C. *Andrew Jackson: His Contribution to the American Tradition.* Indianapolis: Bobbs-Merrill, 1953. An explanation of Jackson's policies, partially made through the use of documents.

Taylor, George Rogers. *The Transportation Revolution, 1815–60.* New York: Holt, Rinehart & Winston, 1951. Part of a survey of American economic history for the general reader and to supplement college texts.

Wiltse, Charles M. *John C. Calhoun: Nullifier, 1829–1839.* Indianapolis: Bobbs-Merrill, 1949. Part of a multi-volume study of Calhoun, this volume is appropriate reading for the era of Jackson's Presidency.

---

## THE AMERICAN HERITAGE NEW ILLUSTRATED HISTORY OF THE UNITED STATES

### PUBLISHED BY DELL PUBLISHING CO., INC.

George T. Delacorte, Jr., *Publisher*   Helen Meyer, *President*
William F. Callahan, Jr., *Executive Vice-President*

Walter B. J. Mitchell, Jr., *Project Director;* Ross Claiborne, *Editorial Consultant;* William O'Gorman, *Editorial Assistant;* John Van Zwienen, *Art Consultant;* Rosalie Barrow, *Production Manager*

### CREATED AND DESIGNED BY THE EDITORS OF AMERICAN HERITAGE MAGAZINE

James Parton, *Publisher;* Joseph J. Thorndike, Jr., *Editorial Director;* Bruce Catton, *Senior Editor;*
Oliver Jensen, *Editor;* Richard M. Ketchum, *Editor, Book Division;* Irwin Glusker, *Art Director*

### ROBERT R. ENDICOTT, *Project Editor-in-Chief*

James Kraft, *Assistant Editor;* Nina Page, Evelyn H. Register, Lynn Marett, *Editorial Assistants;*
Lina Mainiero, *Copy Editor;* Murray Belsky, *Art Director;* Eleanor A. Dye, *Designer;* John Conley, *Assistant*